De
op
of
]
for
jus   t as far a

He acknow   lue of rights language in leg
debate and accept that human rights are not so
political, with social rights language clearly   ving a progressive,
emancipatory dimension. However he says that lawyers   even
well-intentioned lawyers – damage the achievability of the
kin of radical transformation in the priorities of states that a
ger ne commitment to social rights surely necessitates. Virginia
Ma ouvalou argues that social rights, defined as entitlements to
the satisfaction of basic needs, are as essential for the well-being
of the individual and the community as long-established civil and
political rights. The real challenge, she suggests, is how best to
give effect to social rights. Drawing on examples from around the
world, she argues for their 'legalisation', and examines the role
of courts and the role of legislatures in this process, both at a
national and an international level.

Volume 2 in the series Debating Law

Debating Law

General Editor: Professor Peter Cane, the Australian National University.

Debating Law is a new, exciting series edited by Peter Cane that gives scholarly experts the opportunity to offer contrasting perspectives on significant topics of contemporary, general interest.

Debating Social Rights

Conor Gearty
and
Virginia Mantouvalou

WITHDRAWN

·HART·
PUBLISHING

OXFORD AND PORTLAND, OREGON
2011

Published in the United Kingdom by Hart Publishing Ltd
16C Worcester Place, Oxford, OX1 2JW
Telephone: +44 (0)1865 517530
Fax: +44 (0)1865 510710
E-mail: mail@hartpub.co.uk
Website: http://www.hartpub.co.uk

Published in North America (US and Canada) by
Hart Publishing
c/o International Specialized Book Services
920 NE 58th Avenue, Suite 300
Portland, OR 97213-3786
USA
Tel: +1 503 287 3093 or toll-free: (1) 800 944 6190
Fax: +1 503 280 8832
E-mail: orders@isbs.com
Website: http://www.isbs.com

British Library Cataloguing in Publication Data
Data Available

ISBN: 978-1-84946-023-1

Typeset by Hope Services, Abingdon
Printed and bound in Great Britain by
TJ International Ltd, Padstow, Cornwall

Series Editor's Preface

This innovative and exciting series was inspired by one of the best-known philosophy books of the latter half of the twentieth century. *Utilitarianism for and against* by JJC Smart and Bernard Williams, published in 1973, is described on its cover as '[t]wo essays . . . written from opposite points of view'. It is one of the classics of the modern literature on utilitarianism.

Based on this model, books in the *Debating Law* series will contain two essays of around 30,000 words, each developing a strong and intellectually rigorous argument on a topic of contemporary and ongoing debate. The aim is to stimulate, challenge and inform by bringing contrasting perspectives together in the one volume.

The *Debating Law* series offers a forum for scholarly argument and advocacy. It gives essayists the opportunity to make a fresh and provocative statement of a normative position freed from a tight requirement of 'balance'. Although debaters are encouraged to exchange ideas during the writing process, it is not the intention that the two essays will answer one another but rather that each will provide an independent statement of a point of view. Authors may take different tacks and address different issues within the broad topic, and the starting points or foundations of the case on one side may be different from those of the case on the other side. The confident expectation is that the debate format will sharpen issues, and highlight areas of both agreement and disagreement, in an effective and illuminating way.

The *Debating Law* series is designed for a wide readership. The aim is that each essay should be self-contained, accessibly written and only lightly footnoted. Books in the series will be valuable for those coming to the topic for the first time and also for the experienced reader seeking a stimulating, thought-provoking and concise statement of different points of view. They will provide valuable resources for teaching as well as lively discussions of important issues of wide current interest.

Peter Cane

Acknowledgments—
Virginia Mantouvalou

It has been both a pleasure and a challenge to contribute to the Hart Publishing's *Debating Law Series*. I mainly worked on this book while being a Visiting Scholar at Georgetown University Law Centre in Washington DC, and benefited greatly from the intellectual climate there. I am particularly grateful to my academic host, Robin West, for her warm encouragement and inspiration. I am also indebted to Hugh Collins for reading a draft, asking difficult questions and being steadily supportive, and to Conor Gearty for his unique enthusiasm throughout. The University of Leicester has been a huge support too, not least by granting me an invaluable period of research leave that enabled me to complete this book. A number of other friends and colleagues have commented critically and patiently on drafts. Warm thanks are due to Octavio Ferraz, Dimitris Kyritsis, Stuart Lakin, Alvaro Santos and Charlie Webb. I have also benefited from discussions with Harry Arthurs, Varun Gauri, David Luban, Deborah Pearlstein and Mike Seidman. Drafts have been presented at a Georgetown Law Faculty Workshop and a London Labour Law Discussion Group Workshop at UCL. Thanks are due to the organisers Gary Peller, Nicola Countouris and Diamond Ashiagbor, and to all participants. Peter Cane, the editor of this series, commented generously on a penultimate draft. Finally, I owe much to George Letsas for his constructive criticism and unstinting support.

I dedicate this book to my parents, Yiannis and Mary.

Acknowledgments—Conor Gearty

I am very grateful to LSE for my sabbatical leave during 2009–10 —this certainly helped with getting my part of the book written on time. I am also grateful to Virginia Mantouvalou for having helped me to navigate what is for me a fairly new field, as well as to colleagues at LSE and my graduate students for being a perpetual source of intellectual inspiration.

Contents

Against Judicial Enforcement

Conor Gearty

——————⟶•◦•⟵——————

I. INTRODUCTION

ISTART with the three propositions that lie at the core of my
approach to social rights, a term that I understand to mean
the kinds of social and economic entitlements that are to be
found in the international human rights documents (on which
more presently). The first assertion is that this idea of social
rights is in itself valuable, that such entitlements deserve not
just our protection but also to be respected and promoted. (The
same may be true of cultural rights which are also protected in
international law, but which are not my focus here.) My second
claim is that the value of this notion of social rights lies principally
in the political arena, this being the world in which the good that
these words do can be best concretised or (to use a more bucolic
image) most fruitfully deployed. Third, and following directly
from this second assertion, the least effective way of securing
social rights is via an over-concentration on the legal process,
with the constitutionalisation of such rights being an especial
disaster wherever it occurs. Such a move turns the whole subject
over to its falsest of false friends, the lawyers, a community which
(in this context and however generally well-meaning) amount to
little more than an array of pseudo-politicians on the look-out for
short-cuts to difficult questions and for ways of plying their trade
that are more agreeable to their ethical selves.

Each of my three propositions stimulates in turn the three questions around which the narrative that follows will revolve: Why do we care enough about people we have never met to say that they have a right to the (wide-ranging) sorts of things that we say are entailed in recognising their social rights? What value is there in using the language of entitlement and obligation (that of 'social *rights*') in a discourse—the political—which is so wedded (practically by definition) to the ephemeral, indeed (not to go too far) to the inherent transience of truth? And finally, if we are required to be mistrustful of lawyers while at the same time acknowledging that law does matter, indeed is vital to the enforcement (and therefore the realisation) of political will (which is not disputed), how can we tame the lawyers, buckle their wildness and harness them to good social effect?

In the contribution to the debate about social rights which follows, I will often seem to have it in for lawyers in general, and for the social rights litigation-enthusiasts among them in particular. This is the opposite of the truth. Such lawyers are often marvellous people, fiercely bright, immensely well-educated, attractively confident about their judgments, and driven by a zeal to do good which they see (and rightly see, from their point of view anyway) as marking them out from the commercially-driven types by whom they are surrounded. They want to make the world a better place and are determined to use their professional skills to do so. It is not their motive that is disturbing but rather the tools that they choose for the job. Law is simply not good at securing the kinds of changes we need to make if we are serious (as we ought to be) about embedding social rights in our culture. It is politically insensitive and sociologically illiterate, and no end of excellence on the part of its well-meaning practitioners can change these brute facts. There will be more on the lawyers later, but first we need to clear some ground by identifying why our subject matters and why politics is central to its success.

II. WHY CARE?

In times past it was easy to grasp why we both care for others and ought to care for them: it was God's direction. This was so whether or not we rooted our faith in Christianity, in Islam or in one or other of the religions of the world. Each of these ancient structures of belief shares the characteristic of exhorting us to be good, not only to our families and friends (which is easy) but to strangers as well. For those who still take this faith-based approach to the world, social rights may not be necessary—other words and phrases being able to do just as well—but they do come easily as a neat and conveniently contemporary way of capturing one of the terrestrial offshoots of our God ordained responsibility. The Pope regularly attracts opprobrium in the secularised West for his criticism of 'gay marriages' and of laws prohibiting discrimination against homosexuals, but such incendiary remarks are usually accompanied by sentiments about social justice and human rights that make him seem like a traditional social democrat (albeit these are usually drowned out in the furore that his other comments cannot help but generate).[1] The same is often the case with Islam, whose stipulations on charity rarely receive the same attention as the line taken by this or that radical mullah on military jihad.

In truth, much of the Global North has secularised to the point where its peoples are either disengaged from traditional religion or (even if they are not) are not inclined any more to allow religious duty and practice to define their conduct in the public space. This is not to say that faith-perspectives have no say in these societies—Britain has an established Anglican church and the European Union provides plenty of evidence of its Christian origins, while great numbers of Americans are rigorously evangelical in their approach to life. Rather it is to acknowledge that right conduct is

---

[1] See Pope Benedict XVI, *The Human Person, the Heart of Peace* (World Day of Peace, 1 January 2007); J Mahoney, *The Challenge of Human Rights. Origin, Development and Significance* (Oxford, Blackwell, 2007).

no longer determined solely or exclusively by religious attitudes, that a gap has opened up between what (if anything) people believe and the content of the law that regulates how they behave. This leaves an ethical space that needs to be filled when it comes to identifying motives for public action in this kind of post-religious environment, particularly when the conduct being sought to be supported and explained involves reaching out to (and assisting) strangers.

Secular society has always had great difficulty with absolutes of any sort, a scepticism that extends to a reluctance to explore any of the supposed ethical foundations that might lie at its core. The inclination to feel for others, to care about their situation and to act to improve their lot has survived the decline of religion in such cultures—it is fair to say that the people of such places display strong humanitarian concerns, many of them engaging in good works around the world, responding with generosity to disaster appeals and supporting large-scale campaigns, such as those recently aimed at debt relief and poverty reduction in the developing world. To such people, the idea of 'social rights' as the encapsulation of the entitlement that others have to their acting in this way comes perfectly naturally. It may be that this is just the death rattle of organised religion, likely to wither away completely as the memory of what faith-based moral duties once necessitated is gradually forgotten. Or something else might be going on, something deeper and more fundamentally part of what is entailed in our being human, of which religion is not the source so much as one of its possible reflections, and is now, as religion is gradually superseded, being increasingly expressed in the language of human, and particularly social, rights.

The temptation is to say that the capacity to care and the act of caring reflects an intuition about right behaviour that is at the very core of our humanity, and that this explains their universality across the world and their persistence in the face of large-scale cultural change.

A. Doing What Comes Naturally

After decades in the doldrums, when all was thought to be constructed and the human mind a mere creature of the social forces into which the body containing it was born, the power of this kind of intuitive thinking has been making something of a comeback. Its attraction lies in its link to human nature, that we think certain things because of what we are, not how we have happened to have lived, that, as Chris Brown recently put it, what people want is 'deeply embedded in their nature as human beings'.[2] This can be made into an attractive ally of the caring characteristic: many of us want to care for others, feel compelled to do so in a way that seems to flow not from any conscious decision but simply from how we are. However in saying this, how can we know that we are doing more than buttressing what is merely a point of view about the rightness of caring by these appeals to nature: 'it makes sense because we are hard-wired for it'? And if we dodge that hurdle, are we not at very least making the classic error of deducing an 'ought' from an 'is', saying this *is* what we are, so therefore this is also how we *ought* to be; 'we are hard-wired for it, so it must be right'?

Whatever its origins, the power of the human mind has turned this intuition about the rightness of caring into a whole philosophical system. There are several large schools of post-Christian European thought devoted to producing the end-result that we should behave well towards our fellow humans, that is do exactly as Jesus said we should but without relying on him (or is that Him?) for authority. Though they differ radically on what this assumption entailed, both Immanuel Kant and Karl Marx shared this starting point about the integrity of the person *qua* person, and there are many others. A very good recent example is the capabilities approach pioneered by Amartya Sen and Martha Nussbaum, one of the liveliest and most persuasive of the theoretical analyses of morality in a

---

[2] C Brown, '"Human Nature" and International Political Theory' (ECPR Conference, Potsdam, 2009) 4. (Copy with author.)

non-religious setting, and incidentally an approach that—as we shall see presently—speaks directly and convincingly on the issue of social rights. According to Nussbaum, the 'basic intuitive idea' from which all else flows is 'a conception of the dignity of the human being, and of a life that is worthy of that dignity—a life that has available in it "truly human functioning". . .'[3] With 'this basic idea as a starting point', Nussbaum goes on to identify and justify 'a list of ten capabilities as central requirements of a life with dignity'.[4] Precisely how many there are or what exactly they entail is not central to the discussion at this juncture: what is important is to see how these capabilities capture many of the interests that are traditionally reflected in the language of religion, while at the same time transcending the institutional baggage and power structures of such faith-based organisations. So, it is not at all surprising that some of Nussbaum's fundamental capabilities reflect the drivers behind the urge to care: the capability of 'emotions', for example, with its focus on being able to develop attachments, and the capacity (under 'affiliation') 'to recognise and show concern for other human beings'.[5]

The moral force in all this is entirely clear to her and to those who adopt her approach:

> The idea of capabilities all on its own does not yet express the idea of an urgent entitlement based on justice. However, the capabilities approach makes this idea of a fundamental entitlement clear by arguing that the central human capabilities are not simply desirable social goals, but urgent entitlements grounded in justice.[6]

But why are these goals even desirable, much less obligatory? Why care about justice at all? What is persuasive about it to those who do not feel as Nussbaum does, those who resist pushing the

---

[3] M Nussbaum, *Frontiers of Justice* (Cambridge, Harvard University Press, 2006) 74, with the quote being from Marx's 1844 *Economic and Philosophical Manuscripts*, accessible at K Marx—Early writings, 1975—http://wehavephotoshop.com (last accessed 27 April 2010).

[4] Nussbaum, *Frontiers of Justice* (2006) 75.

[5] ibid 77.

[6] ibid 290.

dignity of all to the forefront of their minds, who are happier with self, kith and kin? Here the work trails off a bit, back into intuition and into a kind of post-religious hyperbole about 'its starting point' being rooted in 'a basic wonder at living beings, and a wish for their flourishing, and for a world in which creatures of many types flourish'.[7] The capabilities approach 'wants to see each thing flourish as the sort of thing it is'[8] and this is why it pushes for cooperation, the best means available of securing the 'prevention of the blighting of valuable natural powers'.[9] But can this mix of a secular Sermon on the Mount, St Francis and a kind of pantheistic Darwinism pull off the trick of turning what we all agree we would like to see into something that ought to happen as a matter of right?

Clearly there is more to the human species—indeed to any species—than an instinct to support others, but it is surely right that such an inclination does exist and unravelling it further can drive us closer to the core of Nussbaum's sense of wonder, in the process telling us more about why we care, and therefore (as we shall see) about the importance of social rights, the formula through which (not to anticipate too much) care is articulated in much of the secular world today.

If we think of ourselves not as members of a special species but as each composed of a bundle of genes on the look-out for survival, then it by no means follows that in this field we have to commit ourselves to the rather loaded idea of the 'selfish gene'—there are many routes to survival and not all of them are marked 'me alone'. The way we are is not all self-oriented: as Adam Smith put it in 1759:

> How selfish soever man may be supposed, there are evidently some principles in his nature, which interest him in the fortune of others, and render their happiness necessary to him, though he derives nothing from it, except the pleasure of seeing it.[10]

[7] ibid 349.
[8] ibid.
[9] ibid 351.
[10] A Smith, *The Theory of Moral Sentiments*, 2nd edn (London, Millar, 1761) is available on Google http://my.qoop.com/google/xVkOAAAAQAAJ/ (last accessed 27 April 2010). The quote in the text opens the first chapter.

What Darwin allows us to do is locate an insight of this sort within science and then see it as part of an animal (rather than uniquely human) approach to living. Far from being something spilt into us at birth from which we then learn how to behave, 'the building blocks of morality' are—as the great primatologist Frans de Waal put it in his Tanner lectures—'evolutionarily ancient'.[11] Here are some more provocative words from the printed version of one of de Waal's lectures:

> The evolutionary origin of this inclination is no mystery. All species that rely on cooperation—from elephants to wolves and people—show group loyalty and helping tendencies. These tendencies evolved in the context of a close-knit social life in which they benefited relatives and companions able to repay the favour. The impulse to help was therefore never totally without survival value to the ones showing the impulse. But, as so often, the impulse became divorced from the consequences that shaped its evolution. This permitted its expression even when payoffs were unlikely, such as when strangers were beneficiaries. This brings animal altruism much closer to that of humans than usually thought, and explains the call for the temporary removal of ethics from the hands of philosophers.[12]

Following the logic of this, de Waal asserts that 'empathy is the original pre-linguistic form of inter-individual linkage that only secondarily has come under the influence of language and culture.'[13] The way empathetic tendencies like these influence our behaviour is not conscious in the sense in which we ordinarily use that term. Pascal Boyer describes it in his highly innovative work, *Religion Explained. The Human Instinct that Fashions Gods, Spirits and Ancestors*[14] as being

> the same as 'deciding' how to stay upright. You do not have to think about it, but a special system in the brain takes into account your

[11] F de Waal, *Primates and Philosophers. How Morality Evolved* (Princeton, Princeton University Press, 2006) 7.
[12] ibid 15.
[13] ibid 24.
[14] P Boyer, *Religion Explained. The Human Instinct that Fashions Gods, Spirits and Ancestors* (London, Vintage, 2001).

current posture, the pressure on each foot and corrects your position to avoid a fall. In the same way, [do] specialised cognitive systems register situations of exchange, store them in memory and produce inferences for subsequent behaviour, none of which requires an explicit consideration of the various options available.[15]

The intuition to help others that is the product of this evolutionary dynamic, and its offshoot into a more general empathy and outreach to the other that de Waal describes, is clearly close to the desire to achieve the kind of flourishing towards which Nussbaum's capabilities approach is aimed. But of course and as previously suggested, it is not the only feeling that bursts through the human subconscious into our active selves. There are and have always been other propensities at work too, powerful ones that assert the primacy of the in-group over the other, that may start with kin-support but then move quite quickly into hostility to the stranger.

This is where the 'is-to-ought' trap identified earlier becomes especially dangerous. As we know all too well, even today the sense of the solidarity of the group frequently collides with efforts to engage a wider empathetic response to the plight of others. If it is right to help strangers merely because it is what nature causes some of us to do, surely it is also (more?) right to help only our kith and kin because this is what nature (even more clearly) causes us to do? It is surely right to acknowledge that the universalistic tendency is a weak one in comparison with that which directs our attention and solicitude into the path of those we know or at least know of—our family, our community, our nation—and which consequently underpins our hostility to others.

Indeed, it may well be that we learnt morality by bonding with those we knew, thereby rooting such mutuality at least partly in a shared antipathy to the outsider. If so, then as de Waal puts it, 'the profound irony is that our noblest achievement—morality—has evolutionary ties to our basest behaviour—warfare'.[16] As a mere secondary growth, therefore, a spin-off without direct evolutionary

---

[15] ibid 209.
[16] de Waal *Primates and Philosophers* (2006) 55.

purpose, it may well be that empathy for the outsider will always be delicate and fragile, perpetually at risk of being overridden. To maintain a commitment to others (even within one's own community) is not easy. The reach towards the other is certainly at its strongest where close family is concerned, but gets progressively weaker as it moves away from our direct relations into wider kin and then into community and then even further afield.

How, then, has the wider impulse survived? According to the philosopher Philip Kitcher, with the emergence of language,

> there began a process of cultural evolution. Different small bands of human beings tried out various sets of normative resources—rules, stories, myths, images, and more—to define the way in which 'we' live. Some of these were more popular with neighbours and with descendent groups, perhaps because they offered greater reproductive success, more likely because they made for smoother societies, greater harmony, and increased cooperation. The most successful ones were transmitted across generations, appearing in fragmentary ways in the first documents we have, the addenda to law codes of societies in Mesopotamia.[17]

The law codes mentioned here are one of a number of what Pascal Boyer has very helpfully described as 'commitment gadgets'[18] with which we have tried to tie ourselves down to follow the better (long-term) part of our nature. The point here is about a spin-off from mutual reciprocity that then develops a new head of steam as society evolves and the attractiveness of harmony and smoothness over perpetual violence becomes apparent. This has a strong explanatory power so far as the authority of law is concerned—but it does not necessarily speak on behalf of the outsider: mutual reciprocity and smoothness more easily produce walled cities than open societies. To look for a commitment gadget that ties us to that better part of our nature marked 'empathy', we need to look elsewhere.

---

[17] P Kitcher, 'Ethics and Evolution. How to Get Here from there' in de Waal (n 11) 120, 137.
[18] Boyer, *Religion Explained* (2001) 211.

This is where we can see religion fulfilling the important function that we discussed earlier, albeit one that secularisation has been robbing of much of its force. (Of course religion can also operate to exclusionary effect but few would deny that many faiths come with an inclusionary dynamic as well.) Literature can work in the same way as well and as recent work on the Victorian novel has claimed, good writing has 'helped us to evolve into nicer people'.[19] And also custom: in a recent book *Moral Relativism*, Steven Lukes speculated that

> Perhaps when we are in the 'grip of custom', we are motivated by moral emotions that are indeed 'natural', or innate, which developed because they helped individuals spread their genes: they sounded alarm bells, offering reliable, immediate responses to recurring situations.[20]

As Lukes suggests, 'Perhaps we "prop up" these emotional responses by elaborating deontological rationalizations with talk of the Moral Law and "rights" and with categorical and inflexible moral rules.'[21] Is it the case therefore that philosophy is to be reduced to the status of a mere flying buttress for the cathedral of feeling? So, is this where Amartya Sen and Martha Nussbaum's capabilities approach comes from—a control gadget put in place by clever people, and believed by other clever people, as reflections not only of their brain power but also—albeit less consciously—of the ethical fuel that makes their brains work in the particular way they do?

B. Committing to Human Rights

When people talk of common humanity, Steven Lukes says, '[t]hese days they will speak the language of human rights.'[22] It certainly has its attractions for Nussbaum: 'the capabilities approach is . . . one species of a human rights approach, and human rights have

---

[19] See I Sample, 'Victorian Novels Helped us Evolve into Better People, say Psychologists' *The Guardian* (15 January 2009) 4.
[20] S Lukes, *Moral Relativism* (London, Profile Books, 2008) 47.
[21] ibid.
[22] ibid 20.

often been linked in a similar way to the idea of human dignity'.[23] We have seen that some of her capabilities are too abstract to be recognisable as rights, but there are others that do easily fit the bill: the capabilities linked to 'life', 'bodily integrity', 'thought' and 'control over one's political environment' capture many of the underlying interests behind civil and political rights, while those encompassing 'bodily health', 'play' and 'control over one's material environment' speak more directly to the sorts of priorities that we naturally think of when we speak of social rights. The intertwined nature of the interests behind various rights is clear from the way in which these inevitably broad capabilities are further fleshed out: under the remit of the 'material environment', for example, is to be found '[b]eing able to hold property . . ., having the right to seek employment on an equal basis with others, having the freedom from unwarranted search and seizure' and through labour 'being able to work as a human being, exercising practical reason and entering into meaningful relationships of mutual recognition with other workers'.[24]

In our contemporary culture, human rights is the best 'commitment gadget' available to those whose life project or immediate ethical task is the generalisation of the propensity to help the other into something beyond kin, beyond immediate community, beyond nation even, into the world at large. It is the habit of mind that flows from the far-seeing activist's capacity to grasp that in our shrunken world we are all affected by the actions of each other: the island people whose homes are destroyed by an inundation precipitated by first world greed and recklessness are the contemporary equivalent of the newly arrived neighbour whom some grunting but imaginatively-wired pre-linguistic human types thought it better to befriend and help rather than to kill. The term human rights works so well to capture this feeling because it is multi-purpose: seeming to make sense at the level of morality ('here is why you ought to help the stranger'), in the realm of politics ('they have a human right to this or a human right

[23] Nussbaum *Frontiers of Justice* (2006) 78.
[24] ibid 77–78.

to that—therefore arrangements must be made for them to get it'), and in the sphere of law ('the right is set out in the Charter or the covenant or in the constitution that our forefathers created to keep us in check').

In a way that directly echoes de Waal's insight about the connection between violence and morality, human rights has been born out of warfare, the Universal Declaration of Human Rights agreed in 1948 being a conscious rearticulation of ethics for a post-war age. When the barbarities of the Second World War exposed the folly of trying to cope without fundamentals, the nations of the world found in the language of human rights a frame of reference for future action which was dependent neither on the old certainties of religion, nor the cruel amorality of modernity.

In its first article, the Universal Declaration sets out its stall: 'All human beings are born free and equal in dignity and rights' and because the human is 'endowed with reason and conscience' it follows that we 'should act towards one another in a spirit of brotherhood'. This sentiment is then fleshed out in a series of large rights-claims which encompass not just civil and political rights (which do not concern us so much here), but the whole spectrum of social rights as well. A good example is article 22:

> Everyone, as a member of society, has the right to social security and is entitled to realization, through national effort and international co-operation and in accordance with the organization and resources of each State, of the economic, social and cultural rights indispensable for his dignity and the free development of his personality.

Also, 'Everyone has the right to work, to free choice of employment, to just and favourable conditions of work and to protection against unemployment' (article 23(1)); 'Everyone has the right to rest and leisure, including reasonable limitation of working hours and periodic holidays with pay' (article 24).

The Universal Declaration also states:

> Everyone has the right to a standard of living adequate for the health and well-being of himself and of his family, including food, clothing, housing and medical care and necessary social services, and the

right to security in the event of unemployment, sickness, disability, widowhood, old age or other lack of livelihood in circumstances beyond his control' (article 25(1)).

This all reads very well but when it comes to the origin of these rights, why they exist in the form that they do, what gives them moral force, the document is oblique, indeed almost coy. It seems that recognition of 'the inherent dignity and of the equal and inalienable rights of all members of the human family' as 'the foundation of freedom, justice and peace in the world', together with a shared 'faith in fundamental human rights, in the dignity and worth of the human person and in the equal rights of men and women', are expected to provide the necessary explanation. However, these are little more than simple assertions, the Declaration's minimal, preambulatory necessities before the plunge into the safer waters of defined rights. The drafters knew enough about the past not to want explicitly to root the obligations they were enunciating in any of their faith-backgrounds. By the same token they did not know enough about themselves (as species-representatives) to see that what they were about was reflexively articulating a deep, unreasoned feeling towards the other that echoed back and forth within what previous generations would have called their souls or (in non-Christian traditions) their spirit.

The rights in the Declaration are the outcome of a process of reasoning that is at bottom rooted in an intuition about what is entailed in being human, which presentiment is then translated into rights via a series of stages of ever-increasing specificity, from this original instinct via basic human values through fundamental principle and eventually into rights. We can afford to be quite relaxed about the philosophical origins of these rights and in particular about whether such explanations work or do not work. The point of the Declaration is not to provide a comprehensive rational explanation of rights so much as it is to throw down barriers against too easy an assault on the better part of our nature by the forces of selfishness and of community partisanship that we know lie within us all (and which the previous decade had so starkly revealed to the Declaration's drafters).

C. Rights, Principles and Values

Recalling Boyer's remarks, quoted earlier, to ask 'why we care?' is on a par with asking 'why we stand?' or even 'why we laugh?': we simply do, so let's see how best we can. On this account, the 'is-to-ought' conundrum simply fades away; human rights are the culmination of a process of reasoning designed to orient us in one particular direction (towards caring for the stranger) and away from another (hostility or indifference towards those we do not know). The idea of 'ought' is one of the ways this lesser strand of our nature protects itself from the stronger natural impulses that surround it. It is an attempt at a trump card that might not be guaranteed to win but which the other side never has: in explicit terms, at least, no one constructs a moral theory about the obligation to be selfish.

However tempting it might be, it is altogether too quick to leap from instinct directly to rights. In a way that is very important to a proper understanding not only of the strengths but also the limitations of the language of social rights (indeed all human rights), the intermediary stages between instinct and individual rights that we sketched at the end of the last section need to be articulated and better understood. Nussbaum worked from instinct through capabilities in order to arrive at rights, but embarking now on the opposite journey, it is possible and perhaps even essential to track back behind the language of rights to explore the principles and values which make sense of rights, which further explain their power, and in doing so provide the linkages between them and the natural instincts which on the argument being developed here are at the root of our subject and which explain both its social dimension and its gratifying ineradicability.

That there is this hinterland is evident from all rights charters with their preambulary invocations of wider social interests, a good example being the prefatory remarks to the Universal Declaration itself, quoted earlier. When politicians seek to introduce human rights based legislation they too invariably do so by reference to higher goals, the community aspirations that make sense of the precise provisions to which they are committed and which their proposed laws are seeking to realise. Judges have been advised by leading philosophers like Ronald Dworkin to search behind the law for the guiding themes that both make sense of the rules and assist in their application. In the absence of this higher order context to frame it, human rights discourse would quickly become anarchic, without any means of resolving disputes between rights or of identifying valid rights claims from bad faith reliance on the language for other, perhaps opportunistic reasons. The simple idea of an instinct to care is not enough. It needs further fleshing out before the concrete sphere of human rights is reached, and this is what principles and values provide. Let us look now at what these are. The two are different, with principles providing us with guides for action (in particular concerning the specification of rights and then of the meaning of such rights once specified), while the idea of values functions at a more abstract level, explaining what lies behind the choice of these (rather than another set of) principles.

Turning first to the principles that guide the framing, interpretation and (where appropriate) legal enforcement of human rights, it is possible to identify three that come up time and again when rights documents are being explained or defended. First is the principle of respect for human dignity, which reflects a commitment to the flourishing of our species as a social animal. We have already encountered it when discussing Martha Nussbaum's contribution to the field. At its most obvious, this leads inexorably to the firmness of the prohibition of the instrumentalisation of the person, reflected in the abhorrence for torture and slavery that is such a feature of all human rights documents. It explains too the importance of the kinds of social rights in the Universal Declaration which were quoted earlier: without these basic building blocks of a successful life no man or woman has the opportunity to properly grasp their chance on earth. It also includes those aspects of the more traditional freedoms of expression, assembly and association to the extent that these also enable us to grow as persons through communication with others. Rather counter-intuitively, the right to respect for privacy can function in the same way, as a device for the development of the full range of a person's attributes rather than the means for sheltering from the world that it superficially appears to be.

The second principle is that of legality. This captures the many important aspects of human rights that focus on law, for example the insistence on the independent adjudication of disputes, the requirement for fairness in public decision-making, and the importance attached to a general right of access to the courts. These civil rights are complemented by those that flow from the third of the great tenets of human rights, the principle of representative government. It is this that underpins the various political rights that are to be found in the Universal Declaration, but also subsequently and with greater specificity in the International Covenant on Civil and Political Rights, as well as in the many regional and national rights' documents that have flowed since the end of the Second World War. The right to vote is for this reason a human right, and the freedoms of expression, assembly and association are historically and rightly seen as taking on a special urgency when they are sought to be exercised in the political arena.

The traditional taxonomy of rights sees them divided sharply into hierarchies, with the civil and political at the top, the economic, social and cultural coming next, and new rights lagging somewhat further behind. Never satisfactory even in its cold war heyday, the incoherence of such an approach has done great damage to the subject by suggesting a foundational distinction between rights where none exists: the fact that we have separate covenants on civil and political rights on the one hand and social, economic and cultural rights on the other is the consequence of geo-politics, not reasoned analysis. One of the especially valuable features of Nussbaum's work, discussed earlier, is her rejection of old distinctions between civil and political rights and economic and social rights in favour of a new framework rooted in capability. This kind of emphasis on underlying principle is much better, with rights being parcelled out or explained or argued for by reference to the feature of human rights thinking on fundamentals that the right being defended or pushed for is said most to reflect and embody.

On this principled account, social rights can be immediately seen to be not on the outer fringes of the human rights movement but rather at its core. Dignity drives rights well beyond the world of the civil and the political. In the same way, democratic communication (to achieve a wider range of protections for dignity for example) can be understood as more central than commercial speech. Also, the connection between the rule of law and human rights can be immediately seen to be taking on a new importance with the protection offered by an independent judiciary functioning as both a guarantee of the delivery of political victories via law and a vital bulwark against the lawless abuse of rights. On this analysis the subject of human rights is a dynamic one, fluid, always open to new rights-mechanisms for the expansion of human flourishing, and less hidebound by the finite rights-lists and institutional structures of the past.

It is our obsession with judicial enforcement (or justiciability as we shall call it here from time to time) as *the* yardstick of legitimacy that has led us to believe that civil and political rights—historically more easily reduced to legal form—are somehow *for this reason alone* more real or more true than social rights. A principled approach wrenches us away from this inclination to fetishise the legal. However, if we accept that these are the principles that ought to shape how we frame our human rights demands and which should rightly be allowed to organise the rights that we already have, then we need to ask the next question which, tracking back once again, takes us one step closer to nature: where do these principles come from?

As we have already anticipated, the answer lies in reflecting on our values, on the sense we have of ourselves as an ethical community, a nation, or a state—what it is that makes us what we are and explains why we act as we do. The production of a set of specific human rights is the outcome of a process in which the set of principles (or guides to right practice) which flow from these values are then further translated into entitlements and obligations.

It is a process of ongoing particularisation; values provide the ethical environment within which the principles conducive to human rights can flourish, making those rights both possible in law and embedded in behaviour. It is at the core of the human rights case that just as the principles identified above are universal, so too are the values that inform these principles. In articulating these values, we get as near as culture can to encapsulating in its practice the propensity to care that is at the heart of human rights.

The first and key value is equality of esteem. This is the commitment to the well-being of each and every person that in its breadth comes closest to the generalised warmth towards the stranger which we earlier described as thoroughly rooted in human nature, an offshoot of the efficient altruism that has served our species so well down the ages. It makes sense not only of our commitment to human dignity but also of our loyalty to the equal participation in government which is so much part of the principled approach to our subject. A linked value is that of respect for freedom, a strong commitment to the idea that individuals should be presumed to be free to pursue their lives as they wish, with controls on their choices needing to be justified and deployed only when essential. The values of transparency and accountability (or, better perhaps, justification) work as abstract commitments to two of Boyer's 'commitment gadgets', mechanisms for making it harder to depart from the core values of esteem and freedom. It is these that make sense of the principle of legality and in turn underpin the rights of access to law and to an independent judiciary that figure in so many rights instruments.

This approach frees us to be relaxed about whether or not we are (as Nussbaum denies she is) reading 'off norms from the way nature actually is'.[25] Brown is surely right when he asserts that 'the results of human evolution neither endorse nor undermine any particular political programme',[26] but what they do tell us is a story of human endeavour that locates social and other human rights

---

[25] ibid 347.
[26] Brown, '"Human Nature" and International Political Theory' (2009) 13 (above n 2).

in a large-scale narrative which, in explaining our beliefs, supports them and, in doing so, enthuses us. The propensities which these values reflect may be pervasive but they are not necessarily prominent or primary. While in some unlucky places on earth they may exist only as a memory for a very few or as an aspiration for a tiny community of activists, they will nevertheless be ineradicably there (however attenuated in practice) because there is something natural and therefore unavoidable about these values.

The outreach instinct may be a minor key in the symphony but it is pleasing to its apologists to see that it is a consistent one. Of course its success depends on how successfully it is embedded in culture: this is the point of Boyer's commitment gadgets. One of the great tensions in human rights generally, and in social rights particularly, lies in the contrast between the supposed universality of rights-talk as embodied in international law and the relative lack of grip of such discourse in many cultures. There is a mismatch between what nations say binds them (international human rights) and what in fact governs how their authorities and people behave: local law; custom; religious practices; national pride; and no doubt much else. This is because there are large gaps in the chain that leads from a propensity to care for others to concretised human rights, and without filling in these spaces—locating and supporting relevant principles and values—the likelihood is that any societal commitment to rights will rarely rise above the flimsy and the uncertain.

D. Summing Up

We leave this section with an answer to the question as to why we care—there is something inherent in us, rooted in our evolution into the species we are today, which equips us with a propensity to care for others even where these others are people with whom we have no relationship or whom we have never even met or seen. The inclination varies from culture to culture and within any given culture from person to person. It is not invariably prominent in any society but it is always present even if on occasion driven into near invisibility by cruel circumstance. A further question is provoked by this reply: given that we care in this natural but fragile way, how can we embed caring in a way that strengthens this propensity to do good while reducing the pull of our propensity to act in damagingly opposite ways? If the answer to that question which has been developed here is thought to be plausible, namely that the most effective 'commitment gadget' to hand at this moment is respect for human rights, then how best should we go about securing respect for these rights and regard for the values and principles that underpin them? Is it to be politics or law?

III. HOW SHOULD WE CARE?

Three important lessons of direct importance to social rights flow from the discussion we have just had, on the origins of our inclination to care for others. First, the use of the language of human rights is an invaluable way of expressing this perspective in a form that is universalist, morally-loaded and urgent. It reaches all the peoples of the world and therefore complements well the studies of evolutionary biology and psychology which are similarly intent on the search for commonalities. The notion of a right carries with it a sense of moral entitlement and this serves the useful purpose of rendering redundant the erection of any distinction between the deserving and the undeserving as a prelude to action. Within the field of human rights, the recipients of the care of others do not need first to have proved their worth—their entry ticket is their humanity. This right treatment is urgent because without it the life chances of those in need of help, their right to a decent life opportunity, may well pass away all too quickly. It is well-known that the poor die earlier, are sicker more often, and are educated less than those of their counterparts lucky enough to be better off in material terms. Human rights capture this sense of the imperative of action.

Our second lesson is cautionary: without a strong supporting framework of values and principles, embedded in society and understood and adhered to across a culture, there is every chance of the language of human rights being drained of its potency, of being turned into little more than a set of hoops that are jumped through by authorities but without yielding any tangible benefit for those for whom it should be a wonderful boon. Human rights talk can be useless if it is simply talk and worse than useless if all it does is rubber stamp unfairness and inequality with the seal of (human rights) legitimacy. Sadly this is a very real threat when human rights are sought to be introduced into a society where powerful actors are resolutely opposed to them, and disinclined to allow their individually minimal propensity to care to extend beyond their family or immediate circle. This is what I was referring to at the end of the last section when I talked about the need for the right values and principles to be embedded in a culture before human rights can be guaranteed the kind of traction they need to succeed beyond the paper on which they happen to be written. As we shall see presently, the risks of this are especially high where the legal is given priority over other modes of expression of human rights ideals.

The third lesson to flow from our discussion directly addresses this second point by reminding us that despite its absolutist appearance, all human rights talk is in truth instrumental—it stands or falls by its fit with the values and principles that underpin it, which values and principles (as we have seen) flow from the tendency to care that is at the core of our contemporary understanding of human rights practice. Knowing this allows us to spot bad faith appropriations of our subject, and also arid legal or philosophical cul-de-sacs down which it is a waste of time and effort to go: our principles and values keep us on the right human rights path.

I am now ready for the central argument in this section: the primary way of embedding human rights generally (and social rights particularly) in any given culture is via the political process. This is true wherever the focus of rights activity happens to be. It does not matter whether it is a small local community or the United Nations itself: human rights are always most effectively inculcated into modes of behaviour when they are reached through, rather than in spite of, politics. Whether we are considering the protection and promotion of social rights at the international, regional or local level, the framing of human rights in political terms is the best means available to us of translating the instincts we have discussed in part two of this essay into real advances for those most likely to benefit from them, namely the poor and the disadvantaged; and this will be shown to be in stark contrast to the judicial alternative which will be the subject of critique in part four.

A. The Rebirth of International Human Rights

The political importance of human rights as the primary means of capturing the values and principles reflective of this caring instinct is of fairly recent origin. In the period from the 1948 Universal Declaration until 1989, human rights had been caught up in a dreary no-man's land between the rival forces of the Cold War, with each side engaged in the deployment of human rights as a kind of artillery shell in a war of attrition. The term 'human rights' was seen, and rightly seen, as hopelessly compromised and abused by the partisanship that had engulfed it, far removed from the values and principles from which, as I argue here, it derives its true rationale.

This all changed when the Cold War simply and remarkably melted away with the collapse of the Berlin wall, releasing the energy for authentic (ie principled) human rights that had been pent up for over 40 years. The idea of respect for human rights became one of the fundamentals of the new global architecture designed to rein in the rampant power of transnational business that had begun immediately to soar around the world with little social democratic, much less socialist, resistance. Under the leadership of Kofi Annan in particular, the United Nations endeavoured to rediscover its commitment to a language of human rights genuinely rooted in the values and principles from which it had originally been derived, rightly seeing this as by far the best ethical underpinning for the new era into which the world was moving at such a fast pace.[27]

---

[27] K Annan, *In larger Freedom. Towards Security, Development and Human Rights For All* (United Nations, New York, 2005) available at www.un.org/largerfreedom/ (last accessed 27 April 2010). For a critical account of the UNs engagement with human rights, see S Moyn, The Last Utopia (Cambridge, The Belknap Press, 2010).

Regional bodies too, such as the European Union, turned to human rights as valuable post-socialist language with which to frame their mistrust of capitalist excess. States liberated from external or (in the case of South Africa for example) internal oppression seized upon human Rights as the best metaphorical flag to hang above their new brand of politics, as a practical expression of the 'third way' of the new politics.[28] For their part, countries with more established polities which had survived the end of the Cold War intact nevertheless found in human rights a language with which to sharpen the radical edge which had seemed to many to have disappeared with socialism. On all of these various political platforms, human rights have been understood in an expansive way, to include social rights. Of course there are risks in deploying this language as well as rewards flowing from its effective use and I shall explore these presently. For now though let us explore this renaissance in the politics of social rights in greater detail, starting at the international level.

The International Covenant on Economic, Social and Cultural Rights (ICESCR) of 1966 might have been agreed in a world mired by US-Soviet hostility, but in its commitment to substantive rights which in turn reflect a real commitment to the betterment of the situation of all peoples in the world, it has a resonance today as the conscience of the age of which even the most devoted of its original supporters could hardly have dreamed. The document is composed of 31 articles. These are preceded by a preamble which deliberately echoes the Universal Declaration in announcing its commitment to 'the inherent dignity of the human person' as the source of rights. It also asserts that 'the ideal of free human beings enjoying freedom from fear and want can only be achieved if conditions are created whereby everyone may enjoy his economic, social and cultural rights, as well as his civil and political rights'. Furthermore, 'having duties to other individuals and to the community to which he belongs', the individual is under a 'responsibility to strive for the promotion and observance of the rights recognised in the . . . Covenant'.

---

[28] A Giddens, *The Third Way and its Critics* (Cambridge, Polity Press, 2000).

Two points are of particular interest in the context of the present discussion. First, the preamble makes clear the aspiration of the drafters of this document that while there might be two covenants making up the international bill of rights, there should nevertheless be no doubt as to the indivisibility of the rights set out in each, that the two covenants (this one and the International Covenant on Civil and Political Rights (the ICCPR) agreed at the same time) should be read as one. The subsequent history of the two shows that this has largely proved to be the case, with only a handful of states having ratified the ICCPR without having also ratified the ICESCR.[29] In terms of the old Cold War divide, therefore, it is simply not true that the world has favoured either over the other; the rights may belong to two different rooms (kept apart in this way, as I have said, for cynical reasons) but they share the same human rights home.

The second point is more complex and has important ramifications for how our subject has unfolded. There is a tension in the ICESCR between theoretical commitment and practical reality that is often exploited by critics of the language of the rights embraced within it. If we have basic rights of the sort laid out in this Covenant, intrinsic to our very dignity indeed, then must it surely not follow that those upon whom the duty falls to acknowledge these rights are required to meet them in full, that a right to X is never a right to half-X, a right to food not an entitlement to the occasional meal, the right to a shelter not fulfilled by the provision of a leaky shack, and so on? The sceptics move from this observation to the general point that because full realisation of rights is often, as a matter of practice, impossible (X cannot be done; proper nutrition is not deliverable; the houses are simply not there for adequate shelter), it must follow that the language of rights as a whole (or at least social rights) should be dispensed with—these are bogus moral claims, fatally undermined

[29]   There are currently 165 parties and 72 signatories to the ICCPR and 160 parties and 69 signatories to the ICESCR. Belize, Haiti, Mozambique and the United States have all ratified the ICCPR but not the ICESCR. Guinea-Bissau and the Solomon Islands have ratified the ICESCR but not the ICCPR.

by the impossibility of their full achievement, and that all they do is bring the whole idea of moral obligation into disrepute.

The preamble to the ICESCR provides the answer to this, making clear that effort is required, that we need to 'strive' for rights, that while we might be born with them, work must be done before they can be said to have been 'achieved'. The idea of rights as an abstract ethical goal towards which we progress, rather than as a set of automatically realised entitlements which we have as humans is straightforward and understandable, and an easy answer to the out-and-out sceptics. However, in an interesting way the critic's point does linger in the back of the mind of the human rights activists who are the frontline strivers for and achievers of the rights of strangers: if these rights are truly moral entitlements, why do we have to work so hard to secure them? Why do we not have instant success with those we are seeking to persuade? Why is it so hard to deliver something of such importance as a set of fundamental human rights?

There is a touch of the evangelist about rights-proponents, a belief that their version of what is right (*human rights*) is something above politics, is truer than the cut and thrust of the daily right and wrong that make up other, merely passing versions of truth. The human rights activist often approaches politics grudgingly, as a necessity reluctantly embraced only because the truth is not grasped as instantly by others as it is by the activist and his or her campaigning friends. Such an attitude to politics makes those who hold it always vulnerable to being persuaded that there are quicker roads to their goals which can avoid all the striving and achieving that human rights work seems to entail in a world that is, to the activist, perplexingly hostile. Because having to do politics at all represents a major problem for many human rights activists, judicial interventions to establish rights cannot help but hover tantalisingly before them as a seemingly attractive (and therefore powerfully seductive) short-cut to a better (because more fully realised) human rights future.

B. Doing Human Rights

This tension between acceptance of the necessity of political work and a hankering after the quick-fix of a judicial *Deus ex machina* is a feature of human rights generally but has become especially evident in the field of social rights, where outcomes have proved stubbornly difficult to achieve in the political domain. In its first framing, this was not as evident as it now is with the ICESCR. At its inception, the drafters were clear in their determination to favour the political. Part three contains the heart of what the Covenant is all about, with the rights that are within the ambit of the document being there set out. In broad terms, these include the right to work (article 6), the right to fair conditions of employment (article 7), the right to form and join trade unions (article 8), the right to social security (article 9), the right to protection of the family (article 10), the right to an adequate standard of living, including the right to food, clothing and housing (article 11), the right to health (article 12), the right to education (articles 13 and 14) and the right to culture (article 15).

The language is very general, without any degree of specificity about exactly how these assertions can be worked out in practice. The drafters could afford to take this approach precisely because there was to be in the ICESCR no judicial dimension to the rights set out; nor was there to be any provision in the document for judicial oversight. This being the case, there was no need to flesh out details in anticipation of the kind of close textual scrutiny that would inevitably have been part of such an adversarial process. Freed from the spectre of litigation, the document could be broad and principled, just as the Universal Declaration had been before it. This firm location of the ICESCR in an unambiguously political context allowed ambition in terms of the rights set out while at the same time (and paradoxically) reflecting the modesty of the Covenant's preamble, noted above, and in particular its acknowledgement that much work needed to be done before the inherent dignity of every human could be fully realised in practice. Far from holding human rights back, this lack of a strong judicial dimension liberated the document, enabling it to occupy the political space in a manner that was both ambitious and practical.

There were three ways in particular in which the ICESCR achieved this. First, while some rights are unqualifiedly idealist in a way reminiscent of the Universal Declaration (the right to social security for example), as has already been suggested many of the rights are tailored to the world into which the ICESCR is sending them rather than into some idealised circumstance where moral obligations are expected to be realised automatically in full simply because they are stated. It is not only in the preamble that we find the emphasis to be not on the perfect end point of human rights compliance but rather on the highly political idea of movement in the right direction. Thus to take two specific examples, article 11 includes a commitment to the 'continuous improvement of living conditions' and requires of states a promise 'to take appropriate steps to ensure the realisation of' the rights there set out. Article 12 is about 'the highest attainable standard of physical and mental health': in other words what can be reached rather than what is objectively required. There is much else in a similar vein, with agendas for progressive realisation being built into the rights so as to bring about what, in the context of the right to education, article 13, refers to as the 'full development of the human personality and the sense of its dignity'.

This dynamic quality to the document is, second, evident in the whole of its second part, given over as it is to what the absolutist might regard as a serious reneging on the human rights mission in the interests of *realpolitik*. True, there are clear prohibitions against discrimination on a variety of grounds including race and gender (article 2(2)) and there is also an important assurance for the equal rights of men and women (in article 3), but these points to one side, the part oozes an air of what might be thought a disturbing contingency from the human rights activists' point of view. Article 2(3) contains a clear trade between universalism and the national interest, with developing countries being allowed 'with due regard to human rights and their national economy' to determine for themselves 'to what extent they would guarantee the economic rights' set out in the Covenant to non-nationals. Article 4 could have been written by a modern utilitarian, allowing as it does rights to be limited 'for the purpose of promoting the general welfare in a democratic society' (albeit with the important and un-Benthamite caveat that the essence of the right itself not be destroyed in the process).

Most significantly of all, article 2(1) does not require of each state party a commitment to the rights as such but only that such a party

> undertakes to take steps, individually and through international assistance and co-operation, especially economic and technical, to the maximum of its available resources, with a view to *achieving* progressively the full realisation of the rights recognised in the present Covenant by all appropriate means, including *particularly* the adoption of legislative measures.

The emphasis is added here to underline the expectation anticipated in the preamble—that the rights are not only to be identified but also (and more importantly) still to be achieved and that the primary means of doing this should be via legislation, in other words the political process.

This takes us to our third point, which is concerned with how the inherently political dimension to the Covenant is further reflected in what it says about how it is to be enforced. I have already noted the favouring of the political over the judicial as an implementation tool. Under article 16(1), state parties must report to the Secretary-General 'on the measures which they have adopted and the progress made in achieving the observance of the rights recognised therein'. These reports are then (under article 16(2)) transmitted to the Economic and Social Council for consideration which in turn passes them on to the Human Rights Council (as it now is) 'for study and general recommendation or, as appropriate, for information' (article 19). The relevant UN specialised agencies may also report 'on the progress made in achieving observance of' the rights (article 18). The Economic and Social Council itself is empowered 'from time to time' to issue 'reports with recommendations of a general nature' on matters pertaining to the Covenant (article 21) and may bring to the attention of other UN organs and specialised agencies any matters that 'may assist such bodies in deciding . . . on the advisability of international measures likely to contribute to the effective progressive implementation of the . . . Covenant' (article 22).

The Economic and Social Council realised soon after the ICESCR came into force that it would not be able to devote itself in an effective way to the labour involved in proper oversight of the Covenant, so it established a sessional working group of governmental experts to do the work. This body, too, proved not up to the job, so in 1985 the Council decided to create an entirely new body, the Committee on Economic, Social and Cultural Rights (the CESCR). Unlike its predecessor, the CESCR is composed of independent experts, with each of its 18 members elected for four-year terms, on the basis that the overall composition of the body should be broadly representative of the world as a whole and not any particular part of it. Starting up properly in 1987 (very well timed, being just two years before the end of the Cold War and the revival in human rights that followed), the CESCR has been the engine of growth so far as the ICESCR has been concerned. Though merely a creature of the UN system rather than of the treaty that it promotes, the Committee has not allowed this to cramp its style, quickly outgrowing its modest origins to develop a wide-ranging and, on the whole, impressive set of monitoring practices.

The current position is that states are required to submit a report on their implementation of the Covenant once every five years, following a template of reporting guidelines prepared by the CESCR to assist them.[30] This report is then considered by a sub-group of the Committee which considers what further information may be required, and poses additional questions to the state if this is judged to be necessary. There is then a plenary session at which the state's representative presents his or her

---

[30] CESCR, 'Report on the Fifth Session' Economic and Social Council, Official Records (1991) UN Doc E/1991/23 Supplement No 3 Annex IV.

government's report. After an interaction with the representative (what the CESCR calls a 'constructive dialogue'), the Committee drafts a set of Concluding Observations in which it will usually lay out its principal matters of concern arising from the report and the interaction that will have followed it, often taking the opportunity as well to make various suggestions and recommendations for change.

The whole process was given an immense lift by the CESCR's decision in the early 1990s to open up its procedures to non-governmental organisations (NGOs). Although they are not allowed to participate in the Committee's dialogue with the states, the NGOs may submit reports and even make oral presentations. The idea was to harness some of the energy of civil society to assist the Committee in its endeavours. There have certainly been significant successes, such as the action that was taken to halt the planned forcible eviction of some 200,000 families in the Philippines in the mid 1990s.[31] The process allows both for the making of ad hoc reports by the CESCR and, importantly,for pre-emptive action that may enable it to forestall breaches of the Covenant rather than simply report on failures. If the Committee does not like what it hears from government, it can even send fact-finding missions to the state concerned to find out more, and it has done this on a number of occasions.

The most important aspects of this system of international supervision so far as the protection and promotion of social rights are concerned are its breadth, its capacity to deal with systemic failure and its commitment to a strongly participatory process. Of course there are weaknesses: the CESCR is over burdened; governments are reluctant to engage properly with its work; the will of the committee cannot be translated into action overnight; and no doubt many others. The spectre of national sovereignty—with the protection this gives underperforming states from scrutiny across the whole of the United Nation's supervisory

[31] See Concluding Observations on the Committee on Social, Economic and Cultural Rights on the Phillipines, E/C.12/PHL/CO/4 (24 November 2008), paras 6 and 8; but cf para 30.

system for the protection of human rights—is never far away. It is hard to work towards moral goals in a political climate in which participants have vetoes on account of their status as nation states, while at the same time not sharing in any serious way the goals of the international agreement (in this case the ICESCR) to which their states have signed up.

It is clearly the case that these matters raise difficult questions of international relations and of treaty enforcement—international politics is complex and slow-moving. The question is what to do about them. Instead of giving up on the political, the right response is surely to deepen the United Nation's engagement with this aspect of its work. To a great extent this is what the CESCR has already done so effectively by carving out a much larger niche than that which was originally planned. In the same spirit, special procedures have been used by the Human Rights Council, building on the work of its predecessor body, the Commission on Human Rights, to push UN activity further and deeper into the territory of often resistant states. Important in this regard are not only the special rapporteurs and independent experts on specific countries such as Cambodia, the Palestinian territories and Somalia, but also those which subject particular areas of human rights to scrutiny.

From the perspective of social rights, among the most important of these functionaries are the special rapporteurs on the right to education, the right to adequate housing, the right to food and the right to physical and mental health; and the independent experts on 'the question of human rights and extreme poverty' and 'the human rights obligations related to access to safe drinking water and sanitation' respectively. The presence of these investigators in places of great deprivation can often open up discussion that has been off the political radar for generations, and this can be true in democratic as well as non-democratic countries: the visit of Raquel Rolnik, UN Special Rapporteur on the Right to Adequate Housing, to the United States in 2009 (after years of being denied entry by the Bush administration) produced town hall meetings and fiery interchanges that both raised local consciousness on an issue on which many remain in denial and gave victims of the country's housing crisis a chance finally to express themselves in a formal, international setting, with human rights being focused inward on deprivation within the United States, rather than (as is usual) outwards on the rest of the world.

C. The Growing Lure of the Legal

Despite all this good work, and the prospect of more, the temptation of the law has become increasingly difficult to resist. The purist ideal of a quick and full fix for a human rights violation is never far from the mind of even the most mature and politically sophisticated of human rights activists, especially since the post Cold War world has proved more resistant to human rights than they might have hoped. It may be that the CESCR was right when it began to allow an aura of judgment to creep into its reports, with suggestions of potential breaches of the Covenant finding their way into country reports soon after the Committee got properly underway. But this move towards a quasi-judicial engagement with the material before it in turn helped generate a momentum towards still more legalisation of the Committee's procedures. The fact of the inability of the CESCR to respond to individual claims of breaches of ICESCR rights by specific states stopped being a natural consequence of a sensible framework of supervision and began to seem more and more anachronistic.

Right from the start, the CESCR had developed a system of general comments which had done much to flesh out the content of the ICESCR, thereby meeting the criticism that the Covenant was too vague to be of general use. From time to time these general comments have been procedural (on state reporting on one occasion, for example, and on the domestic application of the Covenant on another) but they have been mainly substantive, with important statements having by now been issued on a great number of the rights in the Covenant, sometimes in very great detail indeed. This ought to have allayed the anxieties of those who felt that the lack of a judicial arm had held back the kind of deep analysis of the Covenant that was necessary to its continued effectiveness, but it has not been able successfully to do this.

The preoccupation with judicial solutions is not just a matter of the activists' impatience with politics which I have earlier discussed; it is a consequence as well of both the culture in which human rights work is immersed and even (without becoming overly academic) the deep structure of the subject. So far as the first of these, the culture of human rights, is concerned, I need to introduce an idea which has been under the surface of the narrative but which must now be brought into full view: right from its re-emergence at the end of the Second World War, the field of human rights has been very much the preserve of lawyers. This is entirely understandable, given that human rights have found expression mainly in international, regional and domestic legal documents which have of necessity required the sort of expert textual elucidation (frequently in the context of litigation) at which lawyers naturally excel. The UN human rights industry (using that term in a consciously non-disparaging sense) has been peopled by lawyers: they have been prominent in the oversight committees, served as special rapporteurs, and been natural choices as independent experts.

As has been said more than once already, this has been a great credit to the legal profession, proudly sending its secular missionaries into the world to do important ethical work. However, these excellent people have taken with them into the field a partiality for the judicial process which is so deeply embedded within them that they think it to be a reflection of the natural order of things and not a (mere) consequence of how they themselves have been educated, and their subsequent lived experience. For most lawyers, standards are not truly real unless their existence can be confirmed in legal proceedings before an independent and impartial tribunal. The primary model to hand is one that insists that litigation is composed of a dispute between two individual parties overseen by an impartial referee judging the case on the material presented to him or her. So the inclination towards the legal in the arena of human rights inevitably takes the form of an insistence on the need for a mechanism for the judicial resolution of disputes between separate individuals on the one hand and the state alleged to have infringed their human rights on the other. Far from being an add-on or a luxury extra, this is the key measure of the effectiveness of human rights protection so far as many lawyers are concerned.

To add to the activists' desire for the 'quick fix' (a little discussed earlier) and the lawyers' partiality for the legal which I have just described, when we consider the dominating power of the law in this field we have, thirdly, to confront the individualism that is inherent in the very idea of human rights itself. The subject is about nothing if it is not about humans and the singular human at that—it is after all a field in which the term 'human rights' is often thought of as descriptively interchangeable with the idea of 'individual rights'. The rights set out in the UN documents are invariably framed in these particularised terms. Of course there are collective rights, most obviously the right of peoples to self-determination set out in article 1 of both the ICESCR and the ICCPR, and also the entitlements of indigenous peoples contained in the recently concluded declaration of that name to which I return in a moment.[32]

But the whole thrust of the subject is anti-collectivist, anti-utilitarian, and avowedly individualist in its central design, and this is the case with social rights as much as it is with the civil and political rights (albeit for these latter sets of rights it is an easier intellectual fit). It is true that, as we have seen, there are overrides in the name of state interest and also many generalised clauses within the ICESCR (such as article 2(1)) which dilute the range of demands which can be made in the name of these individual human rights. However, such departures from the presumptions of personal entitlement are located firmly within the structure of individual rights to which the document (in common with other human rights instruments of course) is primarily committed. Far from transcending such rights-talk, these exiguous and qualified

---

[32] Declaration on the Rights of Indigenous Peoples, United Nations General Assembly (UNGA) Res 61/295 (13 September 2007).

departures from the norm serve to confirm the predominance of the individualist model.

It is in the interplay of these activist, cultural and structural dimensions to human rights that we find an explanation for the seeming inexorability and the apparent unarguability of the move to the legalisation of social rights to which I have drawn attention. What I have in mind here in particular is the trend towards what I will call the justiciability of social rights, in other words the inclination to regard the meaning and enforcement of such rights as primarily a matter for judges rather than politicians. The concern is not with the fact of law: indeed it could hardly be the issue when law is so obviously essential to the realisation of all democratic projects. Rather it is with reliance on the judicial branch to flesh out and enforce broadly based social rights which are presented to the courts in a constitutional but deliberately vague form.

The issue is acknowledged to be a controversial one. Under the heading 'Giving Content to ESR [Economic and Social Rights]: Justiciability', the leading textbook in the field opens with the statement that 'The accountability of governments and other entities, as well as the availability of a remedy in cases of a violation, are indispensable elements of international human rights law'.[33] The authors acknowledge that the 'response of many participants in the debate [about justiciability] is that the need for remedies and accountability need not be automatically equated with judicial remedies' and that there are indeed 'many other ways in which [economic and social rights] might be effectively vindicated' (including 'administrative remedies, and legislative responsiveness to reports by human rights commissions and the like'). Indeed they go so far as to accept that '[g]reater flexibility and responsiveness of some of these techniques can be better suited than litigation for achieving the goals' of economic and social rights.[34]

---

[33]   HJ Steiner, P Alston and R Goodman, *International Human Rights in Context*, 3rd edn (Oxford, Oxford University Press, 2007) 313.

[34]   ibid.

However, and depressingly from the perspective of this essay, the authors then immediately resile from the more flexible, less judge-centred position to which they appeared to be moving:

> Nevertheless, many observers continue to insist upon the benchmark of justiciability (ie the ability of courts to provide a remedy for aggrieved individuals claiming a violation of those rights) as a true test of a 'real' human right. In addition there are clearly some aspects of [economic and social rights] the promotion of which is best achieved through judicial remedies. For these reasons considerable importance has been attached to whether [these rights] are in fact justiciable and the past few years have seen very important developments in this regard.[35]

Sad to say, the last remark is certainly true. As early as 1998, in its General Comment No 3, the CESCR was turning its attention to legal remedies, albeit in the context on that occasion of domestic implementation of the ICESCR:

> While the general approach of each legal system needs to be taken into account, there is no Covenant right which could not, in the great majority of systems, be considered to possess at least some significant justiciable dimensions. It is sometimes suggested that matters involving the allocation of resources should be left to the political authorities rather than the courts. While the respective competences of the various branches of government must be respected, it is appropriate to acknowledge that courts are generally already involved in a considerable range of matters which have important resource implications. The adoption of a rigid classification of economic, social and cultural rights which puts them, by definition, beyond the reach of the courts would thus be arbitrary and incompatible with the principle that the two sets of human rights are indivisible and interdependent. It would also drastically curtail the capacity of the courts to protect the rights of the most vulnerable and disadvantaged groups in society.[36]

It was only a matter of time before the question of quasi-judicial proceedings before the CESCR itself would rise to the top of the

---

[35] ibid.
[36] Economic and Social Council 'The Domestic Application of the Covenant' CESCR General Comment No 9 (3 December 1998) UN Doc E/C 12/1998/24 para 10.

Committee's agenda. A working group on an optional protocol to the ICESCR was established and an analytical paper by the Chairperson-Rapporteur, Catarina de Albuquerque, reported on the various options, the brief not extending to questioning the principle of such a development but concentrating rather on a non-judgmental assessment of the kinds of protocols that could be produced.[37] Major concerns of the CESCR were the comparison with the protection afforded civil and political rights by the ICCPR which does, of course, contain an optional protocol granting a right of individual petition, and the belief that, without an analogous procedure, the rights in the ICESCR would inevitably be seen as second best or as the poor relation of the more robust rights in its companion convention.[38]

Eventually, on the sixtieth anniversary of the day on which the Declaration of Human Rights was agreed, 10 December 2008, and following the lead of the Human Rights Council, the General Assembly adopted an optional protocol, designed (according to its preamble) 'further to achieve the purposes of the covenant and the implementation of its provisions'. The idea is for it to be possible to submit 'communications' ' by or on behalf of individuals or groups of individuals' who are 'under the jurisdiction of a State Party' and who claim 'to be victims of a violation of any of the economic, social and cultural rights set forth in the Covenant by that State Party'.[39] These communications will be rejected unless 'all available domestic remedies have been exhausted'.[40] The mimicry of analogous judicial processes is evident as well in the other grounds for inadmissibility (a 'manifestly ill-founded' communication, for example, or one that is submitted outside

[37] Analytical Paper by the Chairperson-Rapporteur, Catarina de Albuquerque 'Elements for an Optional Protocol to the ICESCR' (30 November 2005) UN Doc E/CN.4/2006/WG.23/2.

[38] See ibid para 60 where the implications of not proceeding with a protocol are set out in a way that refers often to the ICCPR.

[39] Article 2. Note further in the same article: 'Where a communication is submitted on behalf of individuals or groups of individuals, this shall be with their consent unless the authority can justify acting on their behalf without such consent'.

[40] Article 3(1). (Unless 'the application of such remedies is unreasonably prolonged': ibid.)

the pre-ordained time frame of one year)[41] and in the routine requirement for the author of the communication to have suffered 'a clear disadvantage.'[42] Interim measures may be imposed on state parties on the basis of such communications.[43] In the absence of a friendly settlement, it falls to the CESCR to examine the communication and the state's response to it in closed session.[44] In an effort to control this process, article 8(4) provides that 'When examining communications under the present Protocol, the Committee shall consider the reasonableness of the steps taken by the State Party in accordance with Part II of the Covenant'; and when they are doing this committee members should 'bear in mind that the State Party may adopt a range of possible policy measures for the implementation of the rights set forth in the Covenant'. Recommendations are then made to the relevant state party and these have to be responded to within six months of their issuance.

This is all very well so far as it goes. The protocol now enjoys the support of 32 states and more can be expected to follow. Individual petitions will no doubt soon begin to roll in, and it is to be expected that some good will flow from at least a few of them, with individual justice being done from time to time. The question is as to whether this should be thought a *necessary* feature of securing social rights, especially since the Committee already feels itself over-extended and under pressure to keep up with its current work rate. It may well be that as Steiner, Alston and Goodman say, this is the kind of thing required to prove that the rights under its wing are 'real' as opposed to 'unreal'; or perhaps to avoid the description 'essentially vague and aspirational', as Catarina de Albuquerque suggested in her paper, might be appropriate if the ICESCR were to persist without a protocol along these lines.[45]

[41] Article 3(2).
[42] Article 4. (Unless 'the communication raises a serious issue of general importance': ibid.)
[43] Article 5.
[44] Article 8(2).
[45] Analytical Paper by the Chairperson-Rapporteur, Catarina de Albuquerque 'Elements for an Optional Protocol to the ICESCR' (30 November 2005) UN Doc E/CN.4/2006/WG.23/2 para 60(d).

Is it right, though, to open up this new area of individualised work at the risk of distracting attention from the core activities of the Committee, those which police the treaties and take a broad look not at isolated cases of right and wrong but broadly at state practice? Might there not be an example here of the herd instinct in international law, arguing for a procedure simply because everybody else is engaged in it and also because of the deep assumption in international human rights law that to be serious, protection of human rights has to have a judicial or at least a quasi-judicial dimension?

The frustrating aspect to this is that the optional protocol contains an excellent alternative to the communications procedure but one which must now jostle for priority with its more glamorous, remedial sibling. This is the inquiry mechanism in article 11, to which a state party to the protocol can at any time sign up. Under article 11(2),

> [i]f the Committee receives reliable information indicating grave or systematic violations by a State Party of any of the economic, social and cultural rights set forth in the Covenant, the Committee shall invite that State Party to cooperate in the examination of the information and to this end to submit observations with regard to the information concerned.

Having done this and after

> [t]aking into account any observations that may have been submitted by the State Party concerned as well as any other reliable information available to it, the Committee may designate one or more of its members to conduct an inquiry and to report urgently to the Committee.[46]

Where warranted and with the consent of the State Party, the inquiry may include a visit to its territory.[47] The findings of the Committee are then sent to the state in the ordinary way after which, if it so desires, it can chase the state to see what it is doing and (albeit only after consultation with the state party) decide to

---

[46] Article 11(3).
[47] ibid.

include 'a summary account of the results of the proceedings in its annual report' of its activities under the Protocol.[48] It might be thought that engaging in a few article 11 inquiries would be a better way to expend limited intellectual capital and valuable staff time than in reacting to the communications from individuals that are bound to pour in when the procedure has bedded down.

D. The Lawyers' Bandwagon Gathers Pace

The same movement from the political to the judicial that we have just seen operative at the international level has been evident in regional frameworks of human rights as well. The most obvious example of this has been the European Union (EU). Beginning life as a common market, the set of communities making up what we now think of as the EU broadened its remit to give itself a social dimension as early as the mid 1980s, with the Single European Act declaring that European states were

> [d]etermined to work together to promote democracy on the basis of fundamental rights recognised in the constitutions and laws of the member States, in the Convention for the Protection of Human Rights and Fundamental Freedoms and the European Social Charter, notably freedom, equality and social justice.[49]

What this initially involved was a strong engagement on the part of the European institutions in the pushing of a social agenda via the traditional EU lawmaking mechanisms of regulations and (particularly) directives.

The Treaty of Amsterdam confirmed that the European Union was 'founded on the principles of liberty, democracy, respect for human rights and fundamental freedoms, and the rule of law, principles which are common to the member States'.[50] In the

---

[48] See article 15.

[49] Preamble to the Single European Act 28 February 1986 (29 June 1987) [1987] OJ L/169.

[50] Treaty of Amsterdam 2 December 1997 (10 November 1997) [1997] OJ C/340 art 6(1).

late 1990s, the EU heads of government committed themselves to the establishment of a Charter of Human Rights for Europe as a whole and to this end a 'convention' was set up, consisting of the representatives of various interested parties. Its draft of such a Charter was adopted by all 15 Member States at Nice in December 2000. It is an excellent document from the point of view of human rights (including social rights) in that it sets out in powerful terms an array of rights believed to be at the core of Europe's identity and which are already to be found in other national, European and international agreements. Chapter four of the Charter, headed 'Solidarity', deals with the main social rights: included here are rights to social security, healthcare and consumer protection, as well as rights related to the avoidance of unfair dismissal, collective bargaining and much else besides.

The strength of the document lies in its avowedly non-justiciable character, but despite this the gathering momentum behind legalisation has proved impossible to resist: under article 6(1) of the amended Treaty of European Union agreed at Lisbon and coming into force on 1 December 2009, the Union 'recognises the rights, freedoms and principles set out in the Charter of Fundamental Rights of the European Union of 7 December 2000' which are now to have 'the same legal value as the Treaties'. Furthermore, the

> rights, freedoms and principles in the Charter shall be interpreted in accordance with the general provisions in Title VII of the Charter governing its interpretation and application and with due regard to the explanations referred to in the Charter, that set out the sources of those provisions.

The purpose of this is to ensure that the Charter will be capable of being considered as a source of law by the European Court of Justice (albeit this is a commitment which both the United Kingdom and Poland have sought to resist[51]).

[51] See Protocol on the Application of the Charter of Fundamental Rights to Poland and to the United Kingdom: www.lisbon-treaty.org/wcm/the-lisbon-treaty/protocols-annexed-to-the-treaties/676-protocol-on-the-application-of-the-charter-of-fundamental-rights-of-.html (last accessed 27 April 2010).

No one really knows how much the integration of the Charter into the system of judicial oversight of EU institutions will affect the protection of social rights within the Union. Given the depth and range of the EU's pre-existing commitment to social rights, and its laudable commitment to equality and at least a degree of social justice, it is perhaps more likely than not that the Charter will not divert attention away from the need to continue to push on the political front and not hand everything over to the judges. So why embark on this unnecessary, judicialising project in the first place? (The question becomes all the more pertinent if the judges do take the charter seriously, with such activism giving rise to all the objections to such judicial engagement that I consider in part IV below.)

The impact of a not dissimilar development may be different in Africa. A blizzard of institutional action leading nowhere in particular could well be the fate that awaits rights protection on that continent, despite the obvious and critical importance of social rights in this region of the world. The African Charter on Human and Peoples' Rights (the 'Banjul Charter' after the place, Banjul in Gambia, where it was drafted) was adopted in June 1981, at a conference of heads of state and of government of the Organisation of African States (OAS, now the African Union (AU)). The document contains a strong set of economic, social and cultural rights, as well as various innovative rights dealing with other matters such as the right 'to a generally satisfactory environment' (article 24). When the Charter came into operation in October 1986, the main body responsible for its implementation was the African Commission for Human and Peoples' Rights, consisting of 11 members 'chosen from amongst African personalities of highest reputation, known for their high morality, integrity, impartiality and competence in matters of human and peoples' rights' with 'particular consideration being given to persons having legal experience'.[52] The Commission's role included promoting the Banjul Charter, protecting the rights set

---

[52] African (Banjul) Charter on Human and Peoples' Rights art 31.

out in it, interpreting its provisions when requested to do so by a state party or an institution of the OAU/AU, and performing 'any other tasks that may be entrusted to it by the Assembly of Heads of State and Government'.[53]

Early problems related to a lack of resources and the antipathy towards rights shown by some governments in the region dogged the Commission in its early days. The response to this should have been to strengthen its capacity, with the goal being to build it up into a strong body analogous to the CESCR which, as we have seen, operates with some degree of effectiveness on the world stage. Perhaps inevitably, however, this was not the direction which the critics of the Commission had primarily in mind. Instead, as Rehman has observed, '[l]acunae and other additional limitations within the operation of the African Commission for Human and Peoples' Rights prompted calls' in the opposite, but for readers of this essay now familiar direction, namely 'for the establishment of [an] African Court of Human Rights'.[54]

A protocol soon appeared, adopted in June 1998; and with its entry into force on 25 January 2004, Africa found itself the potential possessor of a regional human rights court. Eleven judges were elected in January 2006 but no sooner had this body been equipped with personnel and a building than it found itself facing the prospect of being superseded by the creation of the African Court of Justice and Human Rights, a new institution emerging from yet another protocol, this one adopted by the AU on 1 July 2008. Still another court, this one with an even briefer life, the Court of Justice of the African Union (itself a creature of a protocol of the African Union, dating from 2003) was likewise to be subsumed into the new body.

When it eventually comes into being, this new court (equipped with 16 judges all 'among persons of high moral character, who possess the qualifications required in their respective countries for appointment to the highest judicial offices, or are juriconsults of

---

[53] ibid art 45.
[54] J Rehman, *International Human Rights Law*, 2nd edn (Harlow, Pearson, 2010) 331.

recognised competence and experience in international law and/ or human rights law'[55]) will have a special human rights section and will have regard to an unusually wide range of documents in its adjudicative work including 'any . . . legal instrument related to human rights, ratified by the State Parties' involved in the proceedings before the court.[56] However, in order to access this powerful court, individuals and NGOs will first need to be able to point to a right of petition having been accorded them by the state against whom they wish to take proceedings: there is to be no automatic entitlement to access.[57] This puts rather a damp squib on the energetic provisions elsewhere in the Statute on the enforcement of the court's judgments which are no doubt intended to reflect the modern feel that it is clearly hoped this new institution will have.[58] With the new court not yet in existence however (ratification by 15 Member States being required),[59] the old court of the African Charter on Human and People's Rights is being permitted to limp along on sufferance and only so long as the AU deems it worthy of continuance.[60]

The real pity in all of this is that the needs of the peoples of Africa seem to have been rather lost in the designing of successive frameworks of ever grander human rights architecture. If a fraction of the effort devoted to creating these institutions had been expended on supporting the Commission and improving its capacity, ensuring its independence and strongly backing it in its engagement with the many egregious human rights abuses that exist in too many of the states of Africa, then it may well be that the state of human rights would be in better health on the continent than it is now. It is not only the unduly cynical who would conclude from this story that it is entirely the result of a

---

[55] Article 4 of the Statute annexed to the Protocol on the Statute of the African Court of Justice and Human Rights (2008).

[56] ibid art 28.

[57] ibid art 30(f).

[58] ibid arts 43–46 and art 23.

[59] Protocol on the Statute of the African Court of Justice and Human Rights (2008) art 9.

[60] ibid art 7.

collective desire to be seen to be enormously busy while in fact doing nothing at all.

Not all regional frameworks have gone the whole way down the judicial route in recent years. The American Declaration on the Rights and Duties of Man (which includes economic and social rights) dates from 1948 and was initially non-binding. The later American Convention on Human Rights was adopted in 1969, entering into force in 1978. Though mainly oriented towards civil and political rights, under article 26 of the latter charter,

> the State Parties undertake to adopt measures, both internally and through international cooperation, especially those of an economic and technical nature, with a view to achieving progressively by legislation or other means, the full realisation of the rights implicit in the economic, social, educational, scientific and cultural standards set forth in the Charter of the Organisation of American States [OAS] as amended by the Protocol of Buenos Aires.

Under the OAS charter as amended, an Inter-American Council for Education, Science and Culture had been set up, together with an Economic and Social Council. These were intended to set standards, issue reports and generally oversee this aspect of the American rights agenda. Very little came of it however. So in 1988, the OAS adopted an additional protocol to the 1969 Convention, in the area of economic, social and cultural rights (known as the Protocol of San Salvador).

This addition required parties to adopt measures 'to the extent allowed by their available resources, and taking into account their degree of development' for the progressive achievement of the rights there set out. The process resembles that of the ICESCR with a strong oversight role for the already well-established Inter-American Commission on Human Rights in this field. While a minor role was anticipated in the American framework for the Inter-American Court of Human Rights,[61] the Commission was invited to 'formulate such observations and recommendations as it deems pertinent concerning the status of the economic, social and

---

[61] Article 19(6).

cultural rights established in the present Protocol in all or some of the States Parties, which it may include in its Annual Report to the General Assembly or in a special report, whichever it considers more appropriate.'[62] This system of social rights protection has not worked as well as might have been hoped, and though the judicial engagement is currently modest, the future may well lead to movement in this direction—the short-cut beckons even here.

E. The Radical Potential of Rights-Talk

The political dimension to our subject has been most evident at the national level. This has been particularly clear in the way that human rights have increasingly become the linguistic home for movements and activists (operating on the national but also the transnational stage, often simultaneously) who have been determined to do their best to defend the interests of the poor, the marginalised and the disregarded—all those, in other words, who have been losers or likely losers in the reassertion of market power that has followed the collapse of the twentieth century's experiment with state socialism. The idea of a national commission for the protection and promotion of human rights has become an increasingly accepted one, with the expectation now being that all democratic states should have such an institution to help keep their governing authorities on the right human rights track.[63] Legislative bodies often have their own committees specialising in human rights[64] and with the decline in the language of socialism, political debates are increasingly framed in rights terms.

Recalling the remarks at the start of this part, here we see the instrumental power of human rights being turned to good effect as the platform for expression of that sense of caring for others which we saw in part II to be reflective of the better part of our

---

[62] Article 19 (7).

[63] See Principles Relating to the Status of National Institutions (The Paris Principles), UNGA Res 48/134 (20 December 1993).

[64] See eg the UK Joint Committee on Human Rights and the Canadian Senate's Standing Committee on Human Rights.

natures. Social rights have been at the core of this approach. Importantly, these are not social rights in a narrow sense of this or that article of the Universal Declaration or the ICESCR, but social rights as an idea, as an inchoate bundle of drivers of human potential. The values and principles that as we have seen frame our subject serve also as feeders for new rights and as means of expression of feelings of solidarity with victims of injustice, whose predicaments are effectively (even if not philosophically or legally) described as involving violations of their human rights.

The way the term has been used to underpin action against poverty is a good example of this very contemporary way of doing human rights. The United Kingdom's Joint Committee on Human Rights has remarked that '[p]overty and inequality are the central concerns of economic, social and cultural rights',[65] observing that 'a rights-based approach' is clearly of assistance to 'government in addressing poverty, and Parliament and civil society in scrutinising its success in doing so'.[66] To the leading charity operating in this area, Oxfam, another advantage is that a 'rights-based approach requires' not only 'a system of policy-making that is accountable in law and open to scrutiny', but a way of securing this that involves 'the active participation of those living within the jurisdiction, especially those living on the margins, whether citizens or otherwise'.[67] The experience of the organisation is 'that the realisation of economic, social and cultural rights can most effectively be achieved with the active participation of those affected'.[68]

The range of civil society groups and local communities that reach for the language of human rights to articulate this need for action and to express the solidarity that flows from collective engagement in tackling poverty is impressive and (though obviously each group and community is very local) truly international in its

[65] Joint Committee on Human Rights, 'The International Covenant on Economic, Social and Cultural Rights' (Twenty-First Report of Session 2003-04, HL 183, HC 1188, November 2004) para 102.
[66] ibid para 106.
[67] ibid, Memorandum from Oxfam UK para 3 (Ev 119).
[68] ibid para 18 (Ev 122).

reach. There are good examples in Wales (the Gellideg Foundation Project),[69] Brazil (the shadow reporting on ICESCR obligations in place since the early part of the last decade[70]) and the United States (the Poor People's Economic Human Rights Campaign);[71] and there are many others.[72] What unites them is not the language of international human rights *law* (sometimes they do not even locate their work in this terminology at all) but rather their use of human rights as an idea, a way of asserting dignity, respect for themselves and an insistence that they too (despite their disadvantage and often their misfortune) deserve to be treated properly. A common commitment to human rights can enable the building of alliances that would be impossible without the sharing of a vision that this term makes possible. What other language could, in the name of the moral imperative of poverty reduction, bring together figures from within civil society, government, trade unions, the poor themselves, and even the Pope (whose position on social rights is entirely progressive, even mainstream[73])?

There is an element of artificiality here about distinguishing the local from the global: in human rights terms the latter is merely a vast agglomeration of the former. The point can be seen from the campaign for indigenous rights, which provides another strong piece of evidence for the dynamic vibrancy of social rights advocacy so long as law is successfully kept at arm's length. The energy for this struggle grew out of the determination of these hitherto marginalised peoples to get themselves noticed, a classic basis for making human rights progress. The politics were slow but inexorable, and ultimately very effective. A UN working group on indigenous populations was proposed by the UN

[69] ibid paras 42–45 (Ev 125).

[70] A Donald and E Mottershaw, *Poverty, Inequality and Human Right. Do Human Rights Make a Difference?* (Joseph Rowntree Foundation, 2009) 25.

[71] ibid 15–16.

[72] See generally, ibid.

[73] 'It is . . . necessary to cultivate a public conscience that considers *food and access to water as universal rights of all human beings, without distinction or discrimination*' Benedict XVI, *Caritas in Veritate* (London, Catholic Truth Society, 2009) para 27 (emphasis in original).

Sub-Commission on the Prevention of Discrimination and Protection of Minorities as long ago as 1981, and this initiative was approved by the Commission on Human Rights and the Economic and Social Council the following year. A draft declaration of the rights of indigenous peoples gradually worked its way up the UN system, with ever-wider processes of consultation producing increasingly supported versions of the document, culminating in the adoption of the Declaration by the UN on 13 September 2007. It would be wrong to mistake the length of time this took for a lack of interest in the subject, or indeed with lack of progress. The process itself served the important function of helping to put the interests of indigenous peoples on the political agenda, often where it mattered most—in the countries in which they found themselves and where for decades, if not centuries, their presence had been scarcely noted. Many states with large indigenous communities (not just Canada, Australia and New Zealand from the Global North but, among others, the Philippines, Bangladesh and India from the coterie of developing nations as well) actively engaged with the UN process, even if not all of them ultimately came down in favour of the finished document.

As Rehman has rightly observed, the move towards this rights agenda took place at the same time as 'the emergence of the international indigenous peoples' movement as a global development'.[74] The final document has strong social rights elements, some conventional but many specifically tailored to the needs of indigenous communities—rights to practice and revitalise culture for example, rights of access to traditional health practices and medicines, and a particularly impressive commitment to ensuring indigenous peoples' participation (through their representatives) in decisions affecting them. Of course, it follows from none of this that anyone can go to a court and secure a court order delivering these rights to them: this is not what the Declaration is about. Rather, the goal is, as the preamble puts

---

[74] Rehman, *International Human Rights Law* (2010) 488–89. The International Decade of the World's Indigenous People ran from 1995 to 2004 and has been followed by a second decade, from 2005 to 2014.

it, to set 'a standard of achievement to be pursued in a spirit of partnership and mutual respect'.

We are back to the idea of uncompleted work, and of the imperative of struggle as a prerequisite of progress. This is why the post Declaration UN processes are so important, the Expert Mechanism on the Rights of Indigenous Peoples, the Special Rapporteur on the Situation of Human Rights and Fundamental Freedoms of Indigenous Peoples, the Permanent Forum on Indigenous Issues and the UN Voluntary Fund for Indigenous Peoples. None reliably delivers any kind of quick fix, but then again none of them is designed to. The point instead is to do the politics, to keep the issue alive and to create a climate within which domestic action on these hitherto marginalised peoples becomes a prerequisite of good governance.

Exactly the same interaction between the local and the global can be seen in our final example of the dynamic and effective quality of human rights discourse in the field of social rights. It comes from the very core of contemporary concerns about capitalism: the irresponsible transnational corporation. The capacity of many developing states has all too often not been adequately sufficient to control such powerful economic entities, with the gulf between state and corporate power being such that the national sovereignty so carefully protected by the UN Charter has had little if any traction when it has come to the protection of the human rights of those affected by the actions of such bodies. This has led to international action in the form first of draft norms on the responsibilities of transnational corporations[75] and subsequently (and more successfully) to the work of the UN Secretary General's Special Representative on the Issue of Human Rights and Transnational Corporations and Other Business Enterprises, Professor John Ruggie. The latter's mandate neatly sums up the breadth and range of human rights

---

[75] UN Commission on Human Rights: Sub-Commission on the Promotion and Protection of Human Rights, Norms on the Responsibilities of Transnational Corporations and Other Business Enterprises With Regard To Human Rights (2003) UN Doc E/CN.4/Sub.2/2003/12/Rev.2.

engagement as that term is understood in the first decade of the twenty-first century: it is inter alia 'to identify and clarify standards of corporate responsibility and accountability'; 'to elaborate on the role of states in effectively regulating [corporate entities] . . . including through international cooperation'; and 'to compile a compendium of best practices of States and [corporations]'.

With his innovative 'protect, respect and remedy' approach,[76] Ruggie has been instrumental in forging a new attitude to the subject on the part of the corporations whose commercial activities bring them within his remit. The Special Representative's work has both reflected progress towards better rights protection within states and facilitated movements in this direction that might not otherwise have taken place. The draft norms had failed through their over-ambitious striving for (quasi-)legal respectability: early on in his tenure, Ruggie condemned them for having become 'engulfed by . . . doctrinal excesses' and being rife with 'exaggerated legal claims and conceptual ambiguities'.[77] The open approach of Ruggie, more concerned with values and principles than with the minutiae of legal or potential legal obligation (while not ignoring either when they have been required) has in contrast proved much more successful.

F. The Necessity of Politics

I am now in a position to sum up the argument in this part. Human rights are authentic when they reflect the values and principles that are rooted in the instinct to help, the perceived obligation to care for the stranger that has been part of the behaviour of our species since the dawn of human time. The idea of human rights

[76] See for a recent report which summarises his approach: Report of the Special Representative of the Secretary-General on the issue of Human Rights and Transnational Corporations and Other Business Enterprises, 'Business and Human Rights: Further Steps Towards the Operationalization of the "Protect, Respect and Remedy" Framework' (9 April 2010) UN Doc A/HRC/14/27.

[77] The story is well told in Steiner, Alston and Goodman, *International Human Rights in Context* (2007) 1404–05, with the quotes from John Ruggie in the text at 1405 (citing his initial report UN Doc E/CN.4/2006/97).

is open-textured. Its content changes as new ways of expressing basic values come to the fore, assuming a human rights shape in order both to capture the essence of what the right is about and at the same time to push for its further realisation in the culture in which the argument for it is being made.

All of this is particularly true of social rights because it is the social that is now at the frontier of rights-talk. Important though they remain, the contention surrounding civil and political rights belongs now to a different era, one in which democratic freedom was disputed and the basic recognition of all of us as members of a common species had yet to be universally acknowledged. There are of course still disputes about violations of these rights, but little discussion any longer about their essence, and little sense either of their being liable to change or expand over time. In contrast, it is the porousness of the boundaries of social rights that are their main strength. The basic ICESCR rights are there for all to see but what they entail in concrete terms and the extent to which they are supported, complemented and supplemented remain open to discussion, debate and further action, at the international, regional, state or even purely local level. Viewed in this way, the framing, detailing and embedding of social rights are quintessentially political activities. We have seen in the course of this part, however, many examples of how imperfect is the political support afforded social rights: oversight bodies are overworked; vital resources are not forthcoming; new rights take an unconscionably long time to assert themselves, both as facts on paper and then (altogether more difficult) as realities on the ground.

The tension in the mind of the typical human right protagonist between the certainty of the outcome that is desired on the one hand and, on the other, the radical uncertainty of the political process designed to bring it about has produced a failure of nerve so far as the development of a mature politics of human rights is concerned. We have seen how the inherent 'defect' in politics—that you can never be sure you will win all you want—has been compounded in the case of social rights activism by the subject's focus on the individual and by the strong engagement of lawyers, and all this has pushed social rights protection firmly along the road of ever greater judicial involvement. It has been difficult for those who truly care about social rights to avoid being tempted into the belief that subjecting rights to judicial enforcement will be the ideal way of avoiding the pitfalls of the political, while securing all the benefits that ordinarily flow from success in such a process.

This explains the momentum towards the judicial enforcement of social rights which, as we have seen in this part, has been such a feature of the post 1989 climate, at all levels of governance. But what is so wrong with that, it might be reasonably asked. Why not have the politics and the law operating in tandem? What damage does judicial enforcement do which so outweighs the victories that it delivers that it needs to be given up completely? We might know all that is good about the politics of human rights, but why is judicial enforcement so bad that it should not even be attempted, in tandem with the politics if need be? These are the questions that occupy us in the fourth part of this essay, when I seek to answer the third and last of the questions with which I commenced this enquiry.

IV. HOW CAN WE TAME THE LAWYERS?

The word is tame, not destroy. Clearly, there is a role for the law in delivering social rights, just as there is in every field in all democratic polities. Stripped down to its essentials, the law—and especially the independent system of judicial oversight that goes with it—is an important (albeit usually last-stop) guarantor of delivery of what the legislature and the executive have committed themselves to doing. It keeps public authorities on the straight and narrow by obliging them both to do what is required while at the same time preventing them straying off into territory that is beyond their remit or into areas which are beyond their powers. In this part, I subject the idea that social rights are best secured via strong systems of judicial protection to robust critical analysis; but first I need to prepare the way by reflecting further on what is the appropriate role for law in this sphere. To be opposed to justiciable social rights is to be neither against social rights nor against legalisation; rather it is to hold to the view that turning the judges into the primary deliverers of social rights is a dangerous, indeed a counter-productive, move.

A. Delivering Rights

Strong judicial interventions are by no means the sole prerogative of systems of government with constitutionally entrenched rights. It is clear that they exist also in countries which favour focused legislation over grand constitutional claims. Courts have a role in such systems in making sure that the legal rights for which the state has legislated are properly implemented. Legalisation is not the same as judicialisation—the first is about guaranteeing the legislature's decisions, the second about handing over ultimate decision-making authority to the courts. Examples of the former include the provision of laundry and cleaning facilities for a man with disabilities (the right to community care/disability rights);[78] the supply of home tuition for a sick child unable to go to school (the right to education);[79] and the guarantee of accommodation to disabled residents of a nursing home which had been unexpectedly closed despite earlier assurances that this would never happen.[80] All of these illustrations are derived from the United Kingdom and they show how it is perfectly possible, indeed on suitable occasions required, for the judges to involve themselves in social provision, albeit (as is clear from these examples) as no more than secondary actors, confirming that to which the state has already committed itself in specific, targeted legislation or policy, and

[78] *R (Barry) v Gloucestershire County Council and the Secretary of State for Health* [1997] UKHL 58, [1997] AC 584.
[79] *In re T (A Minor)* [1998] UKHL 20, [1998] AC 714.
[80] *R (Coughlin) v North and East Devon Health Authority* [1999] EWCA Civ 1871, [2001] QB 213.

ensuring that decision-making authorities meet their obligations.

What the judges clearly are not in such a system are primary decision-makers, taking it upon themselves to flesh out the content of a generalised social right and then imposing it on executive agencies. The latter is what arguably occurred in another (very well-known) English case where an effort was made to introduce what would effectively have been a broadly based right to health via judicial decision. In *R (B) v Cambridgeshire Area Health Authority*,[81] a young girl with acute leukaemia was denied potentially life-saving treatment by her health authority, acting in accordance with its relevant policy. Under the then English law,[82] the defendant had a duty to provide for the diagnosis and treatment of illness so far as this was judged necessary to meet all reasonable requirements. At first instance the judge (Laws J) could not resist mustering the right to life as a support for his effort to force the authority to think again, but this broadly-based approach was condemned when the matter reached the Court of Appeal: the court below had gone beyond its own remit by engaging so invasively with what were difficult budgetary matters that as a matter of constitutional propriety fell within the competence of the authority rather than the judge, however heart-felt the facts might have appeared to him to be.

There can also be no objection to general statements of social rights in a state's basic constitution—and there are, as we have seen in part III, good political reasons why broad visions along these lines can usefully be set out in such foundational documents—so long as such affirmative avowals are expressly declared to be non-justiciable, in other words that they acknowledge themselves to be mere guides to future right conduct rather than entitlements to be delivered by judges. Two examples come to mind of the use of the language of social rights in this unproblematic manner. The first is Ireland, a state which has long had 'directive principles of social policy' set out in its constitution.[83] The national authorities

---

[81] *R (B) v Cambridge Health Authority* [1995] EWCA Civ 49, [1995] 1 WLR 898.
[82] National Health Service Act 1977 s 3.
[83] Constitution of Ireland 1937 art 45.

are there exhorted to 'direct . . . policy towards securing' various ends including the 'right to an adequate means of livelihood'[84] and to safeguarding 'with especial care the economic interests of the weaker sections of the community, and, where necessary, to [making a contribution] to the support of the infirm, the widow, the orphan, and the aged'.[85] Crucially, the same article insists that the 'application of [these] principles in the making of laws shall be the care of the Oireachtas [the Irish legislature] exclusively, and shall not be cognisable by any Court under any of the provisions of this Constitution'.[86]

Taking its cue from the Irish, the drafters of the Indian constitution some 12 years later, likewise insisted that its 'directive principles of state policy' (including aspirations of equal pay and rights to work, education and public assistance) 'not be enforceable by any court' while being 'nevertheless fundamental in the governance of the country'.[87] Lawyers might chafe at the spectacle of a country cheerfully committing itself to unenforceable fundamentals, but in truth the problem is in the law-enslaved eye of the beholder: it is his or her narrowness of view with regard to the political that causes the half-sight which in turn leads to supposed discovery of a contradiction when all that is being seen is merely a wider outlook that with which the viewer is familiar.

B. Challenging Law's Empire

If the use of ordinary law to support particularised social rights is essential and the statement of fundamental principles of policy embracing social rights is not necessarily objectionable (and possibly even beneficial), then the same certainly cannot be said for judicially enforceable social rights of a general, constitutional nature. It is these kinds of rights that invite the sort of intrusion by lawyers that has been what this essay has had in mind when it has critiqued the

[84] ibid art 45.2.i.
[85] ibid art 45.4.i.
[86] See the opening sentences of ibid art 45.
[87] Constitution of India 1949 art 37.

role of law in the promotion and protection of social rights. The UK Joint Committee on Human Rights put the case against such an approach with characteristic conciseness and authority in its 2008 report into the case for a bill of rights for Britain:

> We agree . . . that including fully justiciable and legally enforceable economic and social rights in any Bill of Rights carries too great a risk that the courts will interfere with legislative judgments about priority setting. Like our predecessor Committee, we recognise that the democratic branches (Government and Parliament) must retain the responsibility for economic and social policy, in which the courts lack expertise and have limited institutional competence or authority. It would not be constitutionally appropriate, in our view, for example, for the courts to decide whether a particular standard of living was 'adequate', or whether a particular patient should be given priority over another to receive life-saving treatment. Such questions are quite literally non-justiciable: there are no legal standards which make them capable of resolution by a court.[88]

The Joint Committee went on to elaborate on the three 'most common objections' to justiciable economic and social rights. First it was said that the rights themselves would be 'too vaguely expressed', and would 'only raise expectations and encourage time-consuming and expensive litigation against public bodies'.[89] Second, the move 'hands too much power to the courts and so is undemocratic'.[90] Third, such an adjudicative power would involve 'the courts in making decisions about resources and priority setting that they are ill-equipped to take'.[91]

Drawing on the discussion in part III, I might also add several additional points of objection to these. There is, fourthly, the strong emphasis on the individual that is inherent in the whole idea of justiciability, with its inevitable focus on particular claimants at the possible expense of the wider public interest. This might be laudable in the arena of traditional litigation where two parties jostle to secure

---

[88] Joint Committee of Human Rights, 'A Bill of Rights for the UK?' (Twenty-ninth Report of Session 2007-08, HL 165, HC 150) para 167.

[89] ibid paras 183–84.

[90] ibid para 185–87.

[91] ibid paras 188–91.

a reading of a specific law (or prior agreement) in their favour, but it fits less well when such proceedings are being regarded by one of the parties as a device through which to smuggle into court the interests of thousands of invisible claimants, however meritorious the moral arguments being made via their representative litigant might be. Judges are suspicious of 'test cases', not because they are necessarily opposed to the outcome that the litigant before them is pursuing on behalf of others, but rather because of what they generally regard as the self-evident lack of fit between the narrow realm of such litigation and the broader issues that they are being asked covertly to deal with in such proceedings.

This mismatch is compounded, fifthly, by the inappropriateness of the adversarial model to the resolution of broadly-framed issues of social rights going beyond the litigant before the court. Courts are not suitable places to receive, much less assess, the kind of empirical data and guesses about future trends that should underpin all social policy (including the provision of social rights). This is more than a reservation based on lack of equipment for the job (the Joint Committee's third objection, above); it is primarily an observation on the incompetence of the judicial forum however seemingly well-provided for the decision it might appear to be. The point is that it is not the right site to decide these things and the more you fiddle with its procedures to make it the right place (special briefs on socio-economic data and the like; advice from NGOs; expert evidence on the wider social impact of a proposed ruling; and so on), the more any such tribunal looks increasingly like an executive officer, but without the usual democratic necessities of electoral legitimacy and public accountability.

Without a proper enforcement arm as well, a sixth objection to assigning the development of social rights to the judicial branch emerges. Who is to follow-up the court's decision to see that it has been effectively implemented? What happens when unexpected glitches in effecting a court's orders are encountered? Supposing the court's guesses about the cost of its intervention prove to be wrong, how are the new financial implications to be properly taken into account? As with our fourth and fifth objections, the answer to this has often been thought to be to switch the emphasis to ways in which the court process can be made better, more accommodating to the tasks it is now being asked to do. (This defence of 'confession and avoidance', as seductive to rights-proponents as it is potentially subversive of our entire legal process, is widely canvassed, as we shall see, and I will need to return to it before our rebuttal of the argument for justiciable social rights can be considered complete.[92])

Our seventh objection is broader in nature. Even if the court process was sympathetic and able effectively to deliver social rights from time to time, it is still an avenue down which activists for social rights should not willingly go, however tempting it might seem when contrasted with the long and slow political slog that often seems the only democratic alternative. We are back in the territory of part III of this essay: the resort to law in search of the 'quick-fix' of a speedy delivery of solutions to problems that appear otherwise to be intractable. However, changing the focus to law in this way does not come without cost. Even the most enthusiastically backed of human rights campaigns has only a finite amount of energy, and switching emphasis to the courts uses up organisational time, money and campaigner zeal, strengths that might have been better servants to the shared ideal if they had remained where they were, fighting the good fight in the legislature, in civil society and, if necessary, on the streets. Of course, the two are not binary opposites; but what is undeniable is that a twin-track approach (law and political activism) is very difficult even for well-resourced groups to keep evenly balanced on the campaigning road. With its court-room drama, its arguments and its inevitable individualisation of the issues to hand, above all with its prospect of a clean victory in a campaign that seems otherwise so bogged down in *realpolitik*, the lawyers have a tendency to shove all other travellers off to the side. To recall a metaphor introduced a little while ago, they are not being bullies, just blinkered enthusiasts who think the little bit of the path they see is the whole highway.

---

[92] See below text in para following n 131.

Eighthly, there is a possibility which is very familiar to old socialists but which has faded out of the limelight somewhat since the collapse of Marxist confidence in the aftermath of the Cold War: beware of empowering judges lest you give them an aggressive tool with which to hinder (rather than to facilitate) progress. Here social rights come up full-square against the uncomfortable fact that to be fully realised, their proponents may well have to take on established interests whose power and determination to hold on to privilege is certain to make them dangerous enemies. The achievement of the kind of equal society in which social rights do truly allow all to flourish will not be cost-free, in financial or political terms. Great indeed would be the changes that most societies in the world would need to make to effect the radical transformation required to move to a situation in which all those within their borders truly enjoyed their social rights. Taxes would need to be raised, restrictions on individual freedom introduced, bureaucracies empowered.

The legal obstacle that would be likely to arise would have two aspects. First, there would be the way in which civil and political rights-holders would be able to deploy these rights in order to hinder progress and thereby to preserve their privilege. Under the cover of political speech, expensive campaigns against the 'erosion of individual freedom' would be mounted and these would be certain to enjoy some traction with a general public, which would be at this point by definition schooled in the importance of human rights. Similarly popular would be invocations of the right to property and of the urgent need for 'fair procedures' in the face of executive action that would be vulnerable to being credibly attacked as too speedy and disrespectful of existing interests. The results would be quickly plain for all to see: slums would be cleared more slowly; unnecessarily large compensation would be paid to property owners, thereby reducing the pot available to the poor; taxes would produce less revenue than if the right to property (eg extending to inheritance for example) did not exist.

Whereas the old socialist could happily dispense with civil and political rights entirely (a move that would undoubtedly have disastrous effects in itself, it is acknowledged), the social rights enthusiast cannot do this without thereby manoeuvring him or herself into an impossible corner, one which celebrated its commitment to social rights by extinguishing their civil and political counterparts, an absurd stance to end up being required to take. For years social rights proponents have argued for an approach which assimilates social rights to their more established civil and political siblings. They have done this because they have seen the judicialisation of the latter set of rights as an advantage that they have wanted the former rights also to enjoy. However, the examples given earlier remind us that this holistic approach to human rights works both ways.

The second way in which entrenching social rights within the legal system supports our eighth objection to justiciable rights lies in the nature of social rights themselves, and in particular in the effects that flow from the focus on the individual who is (as I have argued) inevitably entailed in such a move. I am not concerned here with the abstract effects of this individualisation, something which has already been covered above (the fourth in this litany of anxieties). Rather it is with what the powerful can do by way of assertion of their own social rights as an indirect means of resisting the social rights of others. Two well-known examples of this come to mind. Many states wrestle with the problem of privately-funded education as a barrier to the achievement of a truly equal society, one in which social rights are available to all. This issue is a difficult one because of the disproportionate hold the 'alumni' of such elite environments have on the society in which they are to be found. The United Kingdom is an outstanding example of this,[93] and yet because of the existence of the (social) right to education that happens to appear in a protocol to the otherwise civil and political European Convention on Human Rights, anyone seeking genuine reform finds an unnecessary roadblock strewn in their way in the form of a parental entitlement to an education of their choice. Article 2 of the relevant protocol declares that '[n]o person

---

[93] 'Unleashing Aspiration: The Final Report of the Panel on Fair Access to the Professions' (Chair: Alan Milburn MP) (London, Cabinet Office, 2009).

shall be denied the right to education' and then goes on to assert that '[i]n the exercise of any functions which it assumes in relation to education and to teaching, the State shall respect the right of parents to ensure such education and teaching in conformity with their own religions and philosophical convictions'.

This guarantee has been construed by defenders of fee-paying education in a way that they would say not only makes the abolition of these schools impossible, but arguably even prevents the state from making any move to deprive them of the tax-related and other benefits which they have historically enjoyed as charities.[94] Of course, a reformer could and indeed should make strong arguments the other way, about the social damage that such schools do, for example, and the injustice that they arguably perpetuate, but the point is that in doing so he or she is having to pit a known individual's freedom against the merely hypothetical social rights that unknown numbers of currently deprived children would (it has to be argued) enjoy in the future if the freedom of an actual, knowable set of children is limited now.

This is a hard case to argue: it is not an attractive position that the rights of children to attend fee-paying schools today should be sacrificed in the interests of all children attending better (because more socially cohesive) schools tomorrow. The problem lies in the fact that the masses of pupils who would be potential beneficiaries of the change are, despite their likely numbers, less visible as individuals than the named boys and girls (and their parents) who would be being made to suffer now. As was the case with the civil and political rights obstacles just discussed, reformers coming from outside the rights tradition have no difficulty with this—of course the known few must suffer for the future unknown many, and the fact that there is a withdrawal of the privileges of the minority now so as to assist in the future flourishing of all is of the essence of

---

[94] The Joint Committee on Human Rights thought any such change would be arguably justifiable in the public interest and defensible under human rights law generally, but in doing so the Committee did acknowledge that such arguments could be credibly made: Joint Committee on Human Rights, 'Sixth Report of Session 2004-05' (2 February 2005) paras 3.5–3.9.

policy-making: this is exactly what planners ought to be doing. Even the most far-sighted and broadminded of those who embrace the language of human rights have difficulty with this; they are uneasy at such utilitarian calculations. Also, human rights proponents of a more traditional, individualist bent are all the more concerned. Where they happen to be judges, schooled in the application of justice not by reference to broad societal goals but in accord with what precisely configured individual cases before them appear to require by reference of legally enforceable human rights law, then the objections become all the greater.

This is why the courts (to mention albeit more briefly our second example) have historically had such difficulty in so many jurisdictions with the concept of affirmative action, not so much with the partisanship shown to those in groups whom the state desires to support in order to better their chances of flourishing as individuals so much as with the consequent disfavouring of certain others, not for any reason related to themselves but solely on account of their membership of an abstract category of person who is being ruled out a priori: he is a man when a women is required, a white applicant where some other ethnic identity is being insisted upon, a person without disabilities when the job is required to go to one with such disadvantages, and so on.

On whose side in such difficult matters of judgment lies the language of human rights? In the political environment it is possible to look to the future and defend the imposition of short-term disadvantage. However, if the judges are given a front row seat in the management of these difficult issues, the outcome is likely to be very different. I should note in concluding our discussion of this important problem with judicially enforceable social rights that here we are not concerning ourselves particularly with any antipathy the judges or some of them might have towards the policies which are being challenged as breaches of human rights (though such antipathy might well exist). The point flows from the very structure of the rights framework itself which when deployed by the powerful to protect their vested interests can make anti-progressive decisions very difficult to resist.

C. The Bewitching Power of Orthodox Thinking

It might be thought that these eight points operate cumulatively to deliver a knock-out blow against the credibility of delivering social rights by means of a system of legally enforceable, generalised entitlements that are then fleshed out by judges in the course of adversarial litigation between individuals and responsible public authorities. This is to underestimate the herd-like instincts of human rights activists, their desire to belong to their own mainstream even while they are arguing for what they think of as a radical change to the status quo. Bravery has its limits: not even the generally sensible Joint Committee on Human Rights has proved itself immune to this conformist contagion. Having dismissed judicially entrenched social rights in the convincing manner referred to earlier, and in the course of doing so going on to deliver the first three of the objections identified above, the Joint Committee immediately began to resile from the implications of its own position, as though terrified of the isolation its intellectual honesty was in danger of precipitating.

The setting in of the rot is evident in the question posed by the Committee just three paragraphs after its dismissal of the legal option: 'Is there a straightforward choice between economic and social rights as mere goals or as legally enforceable rights, or is some combination of the two possible?'[95]

This sentence sums up what is wrong with so many approaches to our subject that end up succumbing to the siren-call of judicialisation. Why describe the goal of economic and social rights in such disparaging terms? What is so 'mere' about a political programme of embedding these rights in our culture? How can such an intentionally debilitated option stand comparison with the clarity and certainty of unqualified rights that are guaranteed to be realised because they are 'legally enforceable'? Quoting an impressive and well-informed witness before it, Baroness Hale

[95] Joint Committee of Human Rights, 'A Bill of Rights for the UK?' (Twenty-ninth Report of Session 2007-08, HL 165, HC 150) para 170.

of Richmond, the Joint Committee found further support for its retreat in the lure of the contemporary: 'There are modern human rights documents and modern constitutions which do include certain basic social and economic entitlements. It is possible to do . . ..'[96]

Who would ever want to be old-fashioned enough to think such rights not worth having in this form? Having worried itself into a crisis of confidence over its initial position, the Joint Committee then found a solution to its contrived dilemma, in the great virtue of expertise:

> In our view the main objections to the inclusion of social and economic rights in a Bill of Rights are not, in the end, objections of principle, but matters which are capable of being addressed by careful drafting. Having given the matter further attention . . . we are persuaded that the case for including economic and social rights in a UK Bill of Rights is made out . . .. [A] country which does not include social and economic rights in some form in its Bill of Rights is a country which has 'given up on aspiration'. We consider that rights to health, education and housing are part of this country's defining commitments, and including them in a UK Bill of Rights is therefore appropriate, if it can be achieved in a way which overcomes the traditional objections to such inclusion.[97]

None of these fine sentiments requires a shift to the judicial, but it quickly becomes apparent that this is at least partly what they entail. While thenceforth and without further argument to be accepted, the 'role of the courts' is nevertheless to be 'appropriately limited'.[98] In a way that I have already anticipated and which I will return to very shortly, the Committee's answer to the inappropriateness of justiciability lies therefore not in refusing to pursue such a course (which might be thought to have logic on its side), but in permitting it in a manner that is consciously restricted. Thus, on the Joint Committee's view, while the relevant social rights will be capable of being considered when

[96] ibid.
[97] ibid para 191.
[98] ibid para 192.

the courts are interpreting legislation and when they are reviewing the reasonableness of measures taken by government to achieve their progressive realisation, they will not be directly enforceable by individuals. Even within the narrow remit that this leaves to them, judges will be required to take into account a whole range of qualifying factors when assessing whether to allow the rights to bite, including: 'the availability of resources'; 'the latitude inherent in a duty to achieve the realisation of the rights progressively'; 'the fact that a wide range of measures is possible to meet the government's obligations'; and much else besides, including the potentially nullifying exception for any restriction on a right which can be said to be 'demonstrably justifiable' in (broadly speaking) a democratic society.[99]

This is the hemmed in world in which the Joint Committee envisages the rights to healthcare, education, housing and an adequate standard of living functioning within the new bill of rights and freedoms that it believes the United Kingdom should adopt. The laudable aim is to win people over to human rights since these issues 'touch the substance of people's everyday lives' and legislating in this way would 'help to correct the popular misconception that human rights are a charter for criminals and terrorists'.[100] However, if they are restricted and debilitated in the way suggested, how would these rights have such an effect? Stuck in a no-man's land between law and politics, social rights would be capable of being litigated (because the idea of judicialisation is seen as good, or at least inevitable) but such court proceedings would be designed in a way that guaranteed ineffectiveness (because the consequences of robust judicialisation are known to be bad).

In this context it is hardly surprising that the Joint Committee should go on to acknowledge that 'the inclusion of economic and social rights' in this fashion 'would not be a panacea to all economic and social ills'.[101] The likelihood is that it would be an anti-panacea, an inflamer rather than a calmer of hostile attitudes to human rights.

---

[99] ibid.
[100] ibid para 197.
[101] ibid para 198.

All the 'terrorists' and 'criminals' would continue to enjoy their robustly entrenched civil and political rights, with strong guarantees of due process, while the losers in the unfair struggle to realise their aspirations in British society, those without good jobs, in bad housing, suffering unnecessary illness and with their children in run down schools—the very poor in other words—would be being told that their plight was better than they thought because their human rights were in truth being respected, with the laws and executive actions responsible for their situation not being at all objectionable in a human rights law sense. The state had done its best and therefore their rights were protected (in law) even while they were being breached (in fact).

There is a general and not just a narrowly British point being made there. Such a consequence is surely worse than not being able to access rights language at all. At least when there is no pretence of social rights in the law, campaigners have an open field in which to use the rhetoric of rights to achieve real change, to struggle for the kind of specific, funded legislation that generates positive rights adequately backed by law of the type to which I approvingly referred at the start of this part of the essay. To embed uselessly ineffective but nevertheless justiciable social rights into the law is to raise an unnecessary barrier to such an activist move. It allows plausible but bad-faith efforts at suffocation on the basis of superfluity: since the rights already exist, no argument surely needs to be made as to the importance of their achievement. In a society which is profoundly unequal but which sees itself as one which respects the human rights of all, this position has an immense attraction. The lucky rich can console themselves that the poverty of the very poor is not an ethical challenge because it exists *within*, rather than *outside* the legal framework of human rights with which they camouflage their greed, as much from themselves as from anybody else.

This takes us inexorably to yet another objection to justiciable social rights, one whose impact is all the greater the more hedged about the rights are in the foundational document that gives rise to them. This reservation (our ninth) focuses on the debilitating danger of the legitimisation of rights-breaching circumstances through a legal assertion, corroborated by the courts, that the abuse does not in fact exist. This mismatch between the values and principles of human rights is familiar in the sphere of civil and political rights where justiciability has (as we have seen) historically been more the norm than in the field of social rights: the ban, on political speech, that is 'necessary in a democratic society' and therefore in accord with guarantees of free speech;[102] the prohibition of political parties because it is said they threaten to infringe the rights of others;[103] the rightness of large-scale detention of demonstrators at a May day protest because it is accepted that the police had no alternative other than to restrict their freedom and therefore did not infringe their right to liberty;[104] and many others. The law has proved itself adept over the years at assuring many victims of rights violations that their sense of themselves as victims is merely apparent.

This trend is already evident insofar as such rights-instruments have sought to reach across into the social[105] and also in the operation of legislative rights in situations where such entitlements are expressed in a generalised fashion that is more often to be found in the sphere of constitutionally guaranteed rights where abstract entitlements are far more prevalent. This danger of legitimisation is far greater where social rights are concerned because, for the reasons I have already discussed, restrictions are usually wider than with regard to civil and political rights—witness the way in which the Joint Committee's support for social rights takes such an attenuated legal form. It follows, from all of what I have said, that while, for the various reasons already rehearsed, fully justiciable social rights are useless, the embedding of such rights in the law in a half-hearted, unenthusiastic way (practically inviting their frequent override) is even worse. To quote Bentham

---

[102] *R (Brind) v Secretary of State for the Home Department* [1991] AC 696.

[103] *German Communist Party v Federal Republic of Germany* App 250/57 (1957) 1 *Yearbook of the European Convention on Human Rights* 222.

[104] *Austin v Metropolitan Police Commissioner* [2009] UKHL 5, [2009] 1 AC 564.

[105] See eg *Hatton v United Kingdom* (2003) 37 EHRR 611 resiling from (2001) 34 EHRR 1.

in a not dissimilar context, not so much 'nonsense' as 'nonsense on stilts'.[106]

How has such a vague and unconvincing position as that in favour of justiciable social rights come to be such an orthodoxy in human rights circles? Some problems are simply so great that the temptation is to address them solely by means of institutional rather than practical change. The illusion of action is gratefully shared by all those for whom the reality is too challenging to properly address. We saw this in part III when I tracked the endlessly revolving systems of human rights that have come and gone (or are going) on the continent of Africa. Something similar may be at work with regard to the imperative of poverty reduction: the obstacles are very intimidating and the solutions that present themselves so demanding that the busyness of institutional change—of courts, and enforceable rights, and new constitutional guarantees—inevitably appeals to many as a way of seeming to act without having seriously to address the core issues of inequality and injustice that lie at the root of the problem.

The largest crisis facing the world at present is that of global climate change. It might be thought inevitable therefore that this is a field which has also begun to attract its very own community of Panglossian optimists for whom no problem is too severe not to be capable of being resolved by judicial action. Thus, the Joint Committee cheerfully observes that the 'briefest consideration of the right in international instruments and national constitutions shows that the right [to a healthy and sustainable environment] has evolved into one which is clearly capable of legal expression' and that it is an area 'for which a particular legal regime can be devised'.[107] Certainly the principles and values underpinning human rights are engaged by the challenge of climate change, particularly with regard to its likely disproportionate impact on the poor and the otherwise vulnerable. The phrase has potential as a rallying

---

[106] The full essay is in J Waldron (ed), *'Nonsense upon Stilts.' Bentham, Burke and Marx on the Rights of Man* (London, Methuen, 1987).

[107] Joint Committee of Human Rights, 'A Bill of Rights for the UK?' (Twenty-ninth Report of Session 2007-08, HL 165, HC 150) para 210.

cry for social activism, so long as it is not destroyed by vacuously constructed general guarantees whose shallow enforcement in law proves more an inhibition to action than a spur.[108]

D. Answering the Sceptics

How then are these nine arguments dealt with by proponents of judicially enforceable social rights? Needless to say they do not cheerfully concede that they are engaged in a trick of the mind, going about doing good work while (proportionately to the problem in hand) not doing very much at all. Three general rebuttals have proved popular. The first denies the democratic point entirely by saying that judicial supremacism (though it is not called that) is part of democracy rather than a subversion of it. The second acknowledges the difficulties with the democratic legitimacy and institutional competence of court action but goes on to suggest certain changes that it is said will make the courts more effective and therefore more acceptable: we have already come across this argument in various shapes in the course of this essay and need now to deal with it directly. The third riposte returns to the instrumentality of human rights, recovers its primary purpose as a promoter of the well-being of all of us, and points to what are said to be the many examples of countries where social rights have been judicialised in ways that have greatly improved the lot of the people within them. All three arguments can be run together and cumulatively they provide the strongest case for persevering with judicial power in this sphere, even over all the objections that have already been mustered. To complete our argument against legal enforcement of social rights, I need now to address each of these points.

Turning first to the democratic response, the style of this school of proponents of judicial power is exemplified in the work of Professor Sandra Fredman of Oxford University whose recent book, *Human Rights Transformed: Positive Rights and Positive Duties*, is a

---

[108] See CA Gearty, 'Do Human Rights Help or Hinder Environmental Protection?' (2010) 1 *Journal of Human Rights and the Environment* 7.

classic of its type. The result of a three-year research fellowship, the author has absorbed vast quantities of contemporary scholarship— though there is no bibliography, no fewer than 55 people are given 'especial thanks'[109] and many of these have written leading works in the field or (in their capacity as judges) pronounced important judgments, and from the notes in the book it is evident that the author has read all of this material, and much else besides.

The method of argument works in a number of stages which are characteristic of this genre of judge-supporting literature. Since it can never do baldly to oppose representative democracy as such, and as judicially enforceable human rights above the political process appear directly to do this, it becomes vital as a first point for Fredman to show how traditional concepts of democracy (those without judicial power at their core) are in fact rooted in a patchwork of defective theories and as a result invariably fail to deliver. First there is the following description of democracy by a well-known economist and social theorist, summarised by Fredman in the following terms and described by her as 'depressingly close to our current experience':

> The reality of modern democracy is that casting a vote in periodic elections gives barely any real participative power to individual voters. But does this mean, as Schumpeter argues, that representative democracy inevitably entails 'rule by elites'? Schumpeter regards the demos as too inexpert, uninterested, or ill-informed to make detailed governmental decisions. Instead he characterises democracy as a process of elite teams seeking popular endorsement by any means at their disposal. Power is exercised by a coalition of elites, with relative autonomy of decision-making between elections. Participation by ordinary people is necessarily tenuous, and even accountability is attenuated, since 'popular opinion' is as much shaped by political representatives as a response to it. The voices of the media, big business, and other powerful bodies drown out that of ordinary people.[110]

---

[109] S Fredman, *Human Rights Transformed. Positive Rights and Positive Duties* (Oxford, Oxford University Press, 2008) ix.
[110] ibid 34.

Nor, second (Fredman argues), is true democracy well served by adopting the approach of the pluralists, those who 'recast democracy as a process of negotiation and contest between organised interest groups for power'. While this might seem to be better equipped to avoid capture by oligarchies and elites 'because alliances are continuously [being] reconfigured, ensuring that power is not concentrated too long',[111] the reality—gloomy but (as we shall see) essential for proponents of judicial power—is rather different:

> Political pluralism is premised first on the assumption that individuals are able to organise around common interests, and secondly, on the possibility of access by different interest groups. As a descriptive model, it is clearly inaccurate. Concentrations of wealth and power inevitably skew the decision making process in favour of interest groups made up of those with power in society. It is a short distance between this and Schumpeter's description of rule by elites.[112]

In Fredman's view, not even the deliberative approach which 'requires decision-makers to justify their decisions by reference to reasons that all can regard as sound'[113] successfully remedies the defects in the two models just described. The 'substitution of interest-governed action by value-oriented action'[114] entailed in the deliberative model is 'not without its difficulties, both in principle and in practice', not least because it is 'clearly unrealistic to expect that all decision making fulfils the criteria of deliberative democracy'.[115] It follows, therefore, that none of these various accounts of democracy is satisfactory. For Fredman, the truth is that to assert that 'the right of participation is alive and well in the political system' is to base one's opinion on 'both a simplistic understanding of democracy and an idealistic vision of the nature of participation'.[116]

---

[111] ibid 35.
[112] ibid.
[113] ibid 37.
[114] ibid 36.
[115] ibid 37.
[116] ibid 101.

It might be thought that such a critique would lead naturally on to a discussion of the possible ways in which these supposedly defective models of democracy can be improved. For all their faults, after all, each has as its primary attribute the raw fact that power flows from living people, whatever their class, gender or level of expertise, however foolish or inept Joseph Schumpeter and other sophisticated minds might believe them to be. However, the proponents of judicialising social rights need to avoid going down such a route at all costs: as Fredman says, 'even if equality of bargaining power could be achieved, political pluralism is a limited model'.[117] These various critical perspectives are in fact merely staging posts en route to a view of democracy in which the idea of human rights is seen not as in contradiction of democratic decision-making but as central to it: 'The above discussion has suggested that modern democracies are a complex amalgam of individual representation, interest group bargaining, and deliberative procedures. Against this background, it becomes clear that to counterpoise democracy with human rights is a false contradiction.[118]

With this breathtaking non sequitur, we have immediately moved onto stage two of the argument, rooted in the world of human rights.

The shift from democracy to justiciable *social* rights is, however, too bald to be achieved directly; it is necessary to shuffle towards them through the less disputed field of the civil and the political. Many civil rights thinkers have been concerned to delineate models of rights which facilitate rather than obstruct the exercise of the prevailing democratic will, and this has led them to emphasise the importance of political freedom as a way of safeguarding the democratic polity, putting oil in the driver's engine to make a journey possible rather than determining the direction in which he or she wishes the engine to take.[119] Declaring that 'positive human

---

[117]   ibid 35.
[118]   ibid 38.
[119]   JH Ely, *Democracy and Distrust. A Theory of Judicial Review* (Cambridge MA, Harvard University Press, 1980); CA Gearty, *Civil Liberties* (Oxford, Oxford University Press, 2007).

rights duties should be recognized as necessary to constitute democracy and to ensure it functions properly', Fredman accepts that as 'a start' such positive duties should entail 'that elections take place and [that] individuals are free to vote' and also that to 'the extent that deliberative democracy is thought to be desirable' there should additionally be 'a clear role for human rights duties to facilitate deliberation, and to channel decision-making away from interest bargaining towards deliberation'.[120]

All well and good, but then comes the next big leap. Because 'as Rawls acknowledged, social and economic inequalities in a modern democratic State are so large that those with greater wealth and position usually control political life and enact legislation and social policies that advance their interests',[121] it follows that 'political citizenship is not sufficient' and that to 'ensure full and democratic citizenship, it is necessary to go beyond liberal and political rights, to the granting of social rights'.[122] This is regardless of whichever version of democracy you choose to follow: all participants in decision-making should be 'formally and substantively equal'.[123] As 'human rights and particularly positive human rights duties are essential to protect the basics of democracy, *including the socio-economic conditions necessary to ensure substantive equality in the right to vote*', it follows that it is 'a false juxtaposition' to say that the way to improve democracy is 'to improve the political system rather than taking away more power from the people and giving it to the courts'.[124]

It is a beguiling vision of democracy for those social rights advocates disposed to the short-cut of judicial activism over the hard slog of political work. The tension between the two approaches resolves into nothing as the former is repositioned to take precedence over the latter as an essential prerequisite to the latter's very operability. Of course the law is presented as auxiliary to politics or the central tenet of representative decision-making

---

[120] Fredman, *Human Rights Transformed* (2008) 39.
[121] ibid 39 (footnote omitted).
[122] ibid 39.
[123] ibid.
[124] ibid 102 (emphasis added).

would be altogether too openly flouted.[125] However, it is clear
that the political will need to do a lot more than merely explain
itself if it wishes to depart from the social rights agenda set for
it by these democratic theorists: there are to be (in Fredman's
characteristically robust phrase) 'predetermined grooves'[126] within
which discourse must run before it is acceptable to the human
rights judges policing the boundaries of the political; and the
weight accorded human rights principles in assessing the limits of
the political is bound to be very high, since to treat them 'as no
different from other public policy principles would be to denude
them of their intrinsic power as human rights'.[127]

Here is political work as the Cinderella outside the lawyers'
feast, able to labour only in the realms left unfilled by the courts'
view as to what is required not just by formal but also substantive
equality. The advocates of strongly judicialised social rights
invariably defend this along lines similar to those of Fredman,
whose view of the judicial role is that it is entirely legitimate
insofar as intervention by the courts can improve the realisation
of 'three key values behind the democratic ideal: accountability,
participation, and equality'.[128] However, while we know from these
social rights critics all about how defective democratic systems
are in regard to these values, in comparison with courts such
democratic frameworks rank as paragons of good practice.

Since advocates of social rights are invariably dedicated to
equality as a substantive policy outcome, not even the most
unreflective of them can avoid noticing that the court system of
which they are such advocates is itself invariably truly dreadful
from exactly the perspectives from which it has proved so easy to
attack the political. Even Fredman acknowledges that '[l]itigation
is sufficiently expensive, protracted, and framed in mystifying
language, to make it inaccessible to most people'.[129] A 'real criticism'

---

[125] '[o]ne of the aims of judicial intervention is to rejuvenate the deliberative
process': ibid 108. Note it is just one of the aims.
[126] ibid 104.
[127] ibid 104–05.
[128] ibid 103.
[129] ibid 107.

is also that the courts are structured in a 'wholly unrepresentative manner, privileging those with the resources and energy to pursue their grievance'.[130] However, instead of acknowledging that the myriad of systemic weaknesses in the judicial branch in most democracies makes them inappropriate guardians of the 'access to resources' on which 'the possibility of effective participation in politics and society . . . depends',[131] these enthusiasts for judicial power invariably set about reframing the adversarial process to better suit their own theories as to what the judges should be doing.

This is the second of the three ways in which the objections to judicial power are met, what I earlier described as 'confession and avoidance': 'yes we know the courts are not suitable for what we want them to do, so let's change how they operate to make them better at what we have in mind for them'. Judges may not have the expertise to deal with the technical issues that would arise were social rights fully justiciable, but they can be trained in all this, hear more experts in court, and even rely on data prepared by specialist bodies such as the World Health Organisation or the International Labour Organisation or whoever. If judges are naturally conservative, then we can open up the appointment process to secure people better at doing social rights than the current incumbents. If the usual way of doing law in the courts is such a problem, then this can be dealt with by developing new ways of bringing cases, involving strategic litigation, class action, revised standing rules, imaginative kinds of public interest interventions and other kinds of innovations, all designed to make it easier to frame adjudication in the kind of large-scale, quasi-legislative way that judicialising social rights demands. The financial constraint can be dealt with by the simple expedient of an expanded legal aid budget—yet another matter that must be seen as above politics despite its vast financial implications because, after all, it is about protecting 'intrinsic human rights' and not merely a matter of 'public policy'.

There is in all this surely a smack of that over-confidence (or is it arrogance?) against which all human rights proponents need

---

[130] ibid.
[131] ibid 110.

perpetually to be on their guard, that sense that their issue is so important that everything else (whatever it is) must give way before its demands. Perhaps the legal system has been designed in the narrow adversarial way that it has for reasons which are unrelated to social rights but which operate more generally for the public good, by facilitating the peaceful settlement of disputes, for example, or ensuring the proper application of existing law? However, none of this is even allowed to be discussed while the justiciable social rights bandwagon rolls on.

Even if under pressure from these counter-replies to their efforts to meet the objections levelled against greater judicial involvement in this field, the proponents of such a move have one remaining argumentative weapon in their arsenal of replies, and it is a powerful one: experience. Recalling the instrumentality of human rights, the law-activists make a point about the functionality not only of the language of human rights but also of the methods used to secure the universal well-being that lies at the contemporary heart of the phrase. The fallback argument mustered here is that, whatever about these defects in justiciability, litigating social rights works because where it has been tried it delivers these rights and this means better lives for the poor and the powerless and the disadvantaged than they would otherwise have lived. In addition, when proponents of social rights in the English-speaking common law context speak of experience, invariably they are referring to two countries, India and South Africa. So far as the first of these is concerned, the main focus has however been not so much on substance as on how the courts have managed to open up the adjudicative process to accommodate ambitious, socially-based proceedings. These have been dependent on an expansive reading of India's constitutional guarantee of the right to life. Another key issue for India has been the involvement of the Courts in overseeing the implementation of judicial decisions.[132]

---

[132] See Joint Committee on Human Rights, 'The International Covenant on Economic, Social and Cultural Rights' (Twenty-First Report of Session 2003–04, HL 183, HC 1188, November 2004) para 43.

It has been South Africa in particular that has cast a kind of magic over the discussion. It seems to have been the Joint Committee on Human Rights' 'extremely instructive'[133] visit to South Africa that led it to modify its critique of justiciable social rights and come down in favour of the kind of role for the courts in this field which I discussed earlier.[134] Like many UK-based academics and judges, Professor Fredman is herself South African, having completed a brilliant degree at the University of Witwatersrand before coming to Oxford on a Rhodes scholarship. The two countries have very close links, sharing a common language and legal culture. There has been great admiration in the United Kingdom for the changes achieved in South Africa in the legal arena since the ending of the apartheid era, and in particular much of this has centred in progressive circles not only on the Republic's new and innovative Constitution in general, but on its commitment to justiciable social rights in particular. With advocates of the stature of Justice Albie Sachs, it has proved very hard to resist the siren song of justiciable social rights so as to avoid standing accused of having 'given up on aspiration', as that great and persuasive judge so eloquently puts it.[135]

So what exactly is the basis for this admiration of the South African courts, aside from the fact that its Constitutional Court enjoys a wide power to protect and promote social rights? True, the focus here is substantive rather than (as in India) procedural. The evidence from the case law is much slenderer than might have been expected, with just three cases regularly coming to the fore in the literature. In the first, *Soobramoney v Minister for Health*,[136] the Constitutional Court denied the claimant the dialysis programme to which he believed his constitutional right to emergency medical treatment and to healthcare services entitled him. A terminal illness

---

[133] Joint Committee of Human Rights, 'A Bill of Rights for the UK?' (Twenty-ninth Report of Session 2007-08, HL 165, HC 150) para 9.

[134] Ibid, para 171 et seq.

[135] See ibid para 191. The quote at n 97 has two gaps—and in the second of these the Joint Committee quotes Justice Albie Sachs.

[136] *Soobramoney v Minister for Health* (CCT32/97) [1997] ZACC 17, 1998 (1) SA 765 (CC), 1997 (12) BCLR 1696 (27 November 1997).

did not per se count as an 'emergency' and the restriction of his healthcare was a rational judgment based on limited resources and so not a breach of his more general right to healthcare. Neither the judgment nor the commentaries on it recount what happened to Mr Soobramoney after the hearing of the case; but given his extremely grave condition it cannot be likely that he survived for very long unless somehow or other the publicity over the case opened up unexpected avenues of funding. Is it unduly cynical to observe that if he did indeed die as a result of his chronic renal failure, at least he and his family had the consolation of knowing that he passed away with his rights fully intact?

The claimant in *Government of South Africa v Grootboom*[137] appears at first sight to have had a much better result than Mr Soobramoney: she and the other applicants in the case had been evicted from an illegal squatter camp and found themselves living in very bad and unhealthy temporary accommodation in a sports stadium. When the matter came before it the Constitutional Court ruled that the failure of the Government to develop a programme to address the needs of those in emergency shelter, within available resources, was an unreasonable interference with the applicants' right to adequate housing. For all the applause the judgment received, however, the Court's order to the Government—to put a proper programme in place—went largely ignored. The plight of the homeless in the Cape region (from where the case had emerged) remained severe. The Court's refusal to act of its own motion to impose the change that it had required drew criticism from the litigant-activists. A sad end to the affair came in August 2008, with the death of Irene Grootboom, still 'homeless and penniless' according to newspaper reports, but with her social rights vindicated one could be almost forgiven for cynically adding.[138]

The third of the important South African cases tells a more upbeat story than either *Soobramoney* or *Grootboom*. In *Minister of*

---

[137] *Government of South Africa v Grootboom* (CCT38/00) [2000] ZACC 14, 11 BCLR 1169 (21 September 2000).

[138] See www.mg.co.za/. . ./2008-08-08-grootboom-dies-homeless-and-penniless (last accessed 22 April 2010).

Health v Treatment Action Campaign,[139] not only was the challenge to the Government's refusal to provide the anti-retroviral drug Neviropine (designed to stop the transmission of HIV from mothers to babies) successful in the narrow legal sense, it also produced a substantive effect of great importance in the overall treatment of HIV in South Africa. The facts of the case were somewhat extreme, with the denial of the drug being based not on resource or efficacy concerns but rather on an attitude to HIV on the part of senior government ministers that was founded in an approach to the illness which could at best be described as eccentric, at worst positively malevolent in its prioritising of unfounded ideology over basic facts. It is a curious decision upon which to base a very large part of the argument for the efficacy of judicialising social rights: the same result would certainly be reached via traditional public law routes that look to the rationality or reasonableness of executive decisions.

Of course there are other cases here and there to which rights-activists can point; but equally, if that game is to be engaged in, sceptics can point not only to the cases already discussed but to recent sharp reverses for social rights enthusiasts, pre-eminently *Mazibuko v City of Johannesburg*[140] where the constitutional right of access to water was the subject of a very conservative interpretation by the Constitutional Court. The enthusiasts will find this case much harder to explain away than *Soobramoney*, and it will in due course (no doubt) produce the usual heart-felt pleas for more imagination from those whose criticism of almost every judicial decision never seems to lead on to any kind of questioning of whether it is right to continue to argue for such judicial involvement in the first place.

Even a proponent of a court-based approach as enthusiastic as Sandra Fredman cannot avoid the truths about South Africa's experience that—even before *Mazibuko*— increasingly stared her (and other enthusiasts) in the face:

---

[139] *Minister of Health v Treatment Action Campaign* (CCT9/02) [2002] ZACC 16, 2002 (5) SA 703, 2002 (10) BCLR 1075 (5 July 2002).

[140] *Mazibuko v City of Johannesburg* (CCT 39/09) [2009] ZACC 28 (8 October 2009). See J Dugard, 'Judging the Judges: Towards an Appropriate Role for the Judiciary in South Africa's Transformation' (2007) 20 *Leiden Journal of International Law* 965–81.

Only a handful of cases on socio-economic rights have in fact reached the Court, and all have been adjudicated cautiously. Constitutional Court judges are known to have suggested extra-judicially that more positive duties cases should be initiated and sent their way, but the constraints [of the type] outlined above have clearly militated against such actions forthcoming. Public interest litigants take many months and even years to prepare their cases, and then must make their way laboriously through the lower courts before reaching the Constitutional Court. Attorneys report that the sheer paperwork in such a case could amount to up to half a million pages with the attendant expense. On the substance of a case, leading barristers frequently advise great caution in instigating litigation, concerned that the most to be expected from the Court is polite prodding of the State into action.[141]

Since liberating itself from the shackles of apartheid, poverty has emerged as the key ethical challenge in modern South Africa.[142] In India, likewise, the ranks of the poor remain infamously vast.[143] The fact that each country has judicially enforceable guarantees against ending up in exactly the situation in which millions of citizens continue to find themselves should surely give even the most enthusiastic of rights-proponents pause for thought: these kinds of social rights are hardly capable of dealing with challenges on such a vast scale, however active and intrusive their judicial overseers might choose to be.

V. CONCLUSION

The scepticism in part IV of this essay should not be mistaken for cynicism. It is clear that legally enforceable social rights can be sometimes effective, not only with regard to the facts before the judges dealing with individual situations but also across society as

---

[141] Fredman (n 109) 123.

[142] For basic data see http://data.worldbank.org/country/south-africa (last accessed 29 April 2010).

[143] For India the basic information is at http://data.worldbank.org/country/india (last accessed 29 April 2010).

a whole. Such cases can unlock debate and discussion which can then lead to action, and this can happen even where the outcome in any given case is disappointing from a litigant's point of view. The question is whether these occasional victories and sporadic consciousness-raising exercises are worth the effort, especially when the disadvantages of the full judicialisation of social rights dealt are taken into account: the danger of the legitimising of injustice; the risk of erecting unnecessary barriers to social progress; the drift away from democratic politics; the distortion of the judicial process; and all the other objections that have been mustered in part IV of this essay.

Even in its grossly defective state (as the legalised-rights-protagonists would have us believe is the case generally), what is so wrong about politics anyway? The decline in poverty in India and South Africa may well owe more to the fact that both countries are democratic in the old fashioned sense of having voters that matter rather than that there are litigable rights upon which activists can rely. For all its ongoing problems, South Africa in particular has made great strides in poverty reduction since the end of the apartheid era, not perfect of course but indubitably in the right direction.[144] With President Barack Obama's success in enacting a new healthcare law in the United States (albeit now under challenge in the courts), we have a very good example of the power of democratic engagement to achieve change for the better in social rights provision, just as we had in 1946 with the right-less United Kingdom's establishment of a National Health Service. There are countless similar examples across the world of slow progress to reduce poverty through planned, unglamorous political action, underpinned by reliance on human rights as a source of intellectual and popular mobilisation rather than litigation: Thomas Pogge's work on a health impact fund which seeks to secure access to treatment drugs for the poor comes

---

[144] See http://data.worldbank.org/country/south-africa.

to mind,[145] as do current efforts to introduce a 'Tobin' tax on international currency transactions.[146]

The United Kingdom's National Health Service took three years to come into operation and from the start it was dogged by funding problems and (initially at any rate) professional hostility. President Obama nearly lost health reform completely through the death of the senator most identified with the reform and his replacement by an opponent of the President's proposals. Of course politics is a slow business, often poisoned by the influence of money and with seemingly endless setbacks along the way, various pitfalls that seem always to need to be negotiated and concessions made—all of this tries the patience of rights activists and drives many of them into the courtroom in search of a quick route to absolute victory. However, the central argument of this essay has been that such tempting short-cuts are in truth cul-de-sacs, and that there is no alternative to careful navigation of the traditional route, one that when it is successfully negotiated and the finish line reached has carried all its passengers with it to a destination that is both new and real, and where everybody now agrees it is right to be.

If we truly want to act to improve the life-chances of our fellow species-members, then we owe it to them (and perhaps also to ourselves) to do more than merely to seem only to care. We need to resist the temptation to surround ourselves in fine language as a way of obscuring (to ourselves as much as to anyone else) that we are doing next to nothing to change the world of which we say we disapprove. Caring may indeed be part of our nature, but it is through politics rather than the law that we can embed this instinct in our culture and make what is second nature to some of us an assumption about right behaviour that no one thinks to question.

[145] See T Pogge, 'The Health Impact Fund and its Justification by Appeal to Human Rights' (2009) 40 *Journal of Social Philosophy* 542.

[146] The momentum for this change has gathered pace since the economic collapse of 2008: see L Elliott, 'The Time is Ripe for a Tobin Tax' *The Guardian* (27 August 2009) at www.guardian.co.uk/business/2009/aug/27/turner-tobin-tax-economic-policy (last accessed 2 May 2010).

In Support of Legalisation

Virginia Mantouvalou

———➤•◄———

I. INTRODUCTION

YOU AND I might desire different things. We each have distinct purposes and choose a distinct way of living. I might enjoy travelling to exotic islands, or to remote countries to get to know new cultures; you might prefer to spend your life reading literature, going to artistic exhibitions or drinking in the pub with your friends. We probably cannot convince each other that this or that activity is more worthwhile to pursue, because we each have a different conception of what makes a life worthwhile. There are certain goods, though, which are necessary in order for *any* conception of the good life to succeed. What are these necessary goods? I shall try to identify some by using an example from real life. I am sure that you could come up with plenty of other examples.

Mr Limbuela from Angola, Mr Tesema from Ethiopia, and Mr Adam who claimed to be from Sudan, reached the United Kingdom to claim asylum. Having fled their countries, they hoped that they would at last be treated with respect. In the United Kingdom, however, while their asylum applications were pending, the Secretary of State decided to exclude them from support, for the reason that they did not apply for asylum as soon as reasonably practicable upon arrival to the country. Mr Limbuela had to sleep rough. He was frightened, he had no food, although he begged, and he was cold. Passers-by did not give him anything and the police refused to offer him a blanket. He was in pain because of ill-health. He was provided with shelter by a charity, but a few days later he was asked to leave. Mr Tesema was a bit more fortunate. Following the Home Secretary's decision to withdraw welfare support, he applied for, and obtained, interim relief having convinced a judge that he would suffer in destitution if evicted from his emergency accommodation. While waiting for his asylum claim to be decided, Mr Adam slept in a sleeping bag inside a car park. When it rained, he got wet, and on one occasion he was abused by a passer-by. He was getting ill, and he could not understand why he had to sleep in a car park. Although Mr Limbuela, Mr Tesema and Mr Adam were hopeful when they arrived in the United Kingdom to claim asylum, they found themselves destitute, vulnerable to physical violence and unable to satisfy their most basic needs. They had no right to work while their asylum application was pending. Their situation was desperate.

You and I are not in the position of Mr Limbuela, Mr Tesema and Mr Adam, but we would probably sympathise with them. We realise that living a life deprived of fundamental necessities like shelter, food and basic healthcare, is a terrible plight. If we passed by and saw them begging, we might feel charitable and give them some food or coins. Shelter, basic healthcare and nutrition are some of the material conditions that we need, the satisfaction of which many of us take for granted. However, not everyone enjoys access to these goods, as the above examples remind us.

Situations like that faced by Mr Limbuela, Mr Tesema and Mr Adam, are commonly described nowadays as violations of human rights. Although the notion of a violation of rights is often used to describe an injustice, there is a big discrepancy in the legal protection of some of these rights, the so-called 'social and economic rights', such as the right to healthcare and the right to housing, as opposed to 'civil and political rights', such as the right to life and the right to privacy. It would not be an exaggeration to say that the most pressing questions surrounding the legal protection of civil and political rights—rights which have traditionally been seen as essential for a state that respects its citizens—have largely been settled today. Issues of freedom of religion, the right to privacy or the prohibition of torture have been and continue to be widely debated in courts, in academic literature, in public and political debates. Theoretical disagreement might still exist about certain subtle aspects of the scope of these rights (eg the right to private life covers most of our activities at home, but do we have a right to engage in private activities when we are in public?) and violations persist in the real world. Yet few would contest their universal importance, their weight for individual autonomy, the need to protect them in law and to fight to address their violation in practice. Governments that breach civil and political rights tend to hide their actions. They are aware that disrespect for these rights is condemned by the international community; if asked, they deny, for instance, that they engage in torture or that they do not respect freedom of speech.

In contrast to debates about civil and political rights, debates about social and economic rights are far from settled. The practical implementation of social rights in particular remains deeply controversial amongst activists, academic scholars, lawyers and judges alike. Some activists view social rights as worth fighting for, and employ the language of rights and their alleged violation as an all-encompassing rhetorical device to advance claims of injustice stemming from economic need. Other activists hold the view that there is little chance that social change will come about through 'rights talk'; what we really need is action, not 'vacuous rhetoric'.

Some scholars are passionate about the importance and necessity of understanding the interests grounding social rights and exploring their legal protection. Others accept that the right to housing, the right to decent working conditions or the right to healthcare are weighty moral and political considerations, but dispute their suitability for legal enforcement. Some view them as valid concerns, which should be left to philanthropy. We may choose to give something to the desperately needy, but we may not be *compelled* to do so; a just distribution of resources should follow some conception of desert, so we should not be required to give away our property if we have worked for it. Others believe that the idea that there are social rights is flawed conceptually, because there is no such thing as an entitlement to resources such as healthcare and education. Finally, there are those who dislike the words 'human rights' altogether, both civil and political, and socio-economic; for they think that human rights are overly individualistic: they depoliticise crucial political questions, distract from political struggles, and ultimately fail to combat injustice.

In this essay, I argue for a general legal right against poverty, a right to have one's basic needs met. I suggest that the legalisation of social and economic rights, which encapsulate this general right, is necessary in any decent society and in a just world order. These entitlements are 'constitutional essentials'[1] on a domestic level, and claims of the highest priority in inter-state relations. Political struggles against poverty, expressed through participation in political parties, organisations that promote social justice or engagement in other forms of active citizenship, are invaluable to be sure. The legal protection of social rights, however, is the best expression of how serious we are about our commitment to these claims. Our elected representatives should endorse them and award them a higher status than ordinary legislation domestically, and our courts should hold the perpetrators of their violation to account. Our legislatures and the international community should give social rights a character of high priority; for a deep commitment to social rights through law shows that we care for the well-being of all people, including the weakest and most vulnerable.

The structure of the argument is as follows. First, the essay explores the meaning of socio-economic rights and catalogues their inclusion in legal documents. This survey finds that there is a discrepancy in the attention that the international community and several governments have paid to social rights when compared to their civil and political counterparts. The section that follows

---

[1] I am borrowing the term 'constitutional essentials' from John Rawls, *Political Liberalism*, 3rd edn (New York, Columbia University Press, 2005) 227. Rawls did not include social rights in the constitutional essentials.

argues that this situation is problematic, because the moral weight and significance of social rights is as critical as that of civil and political rights. Social rights are grounded on several values, including values that also support civil and political rights: they are essential for living a dignified life, for liberty and the ability to pursue valuable aims, for citizenship and social cohesion.

The next section turns in more detail to legalisation, by which I mean giving legal force to social rights. The argument is motivated by the belief that if we are seriously committed to the values promoted by social rights, we need to protect them in law. Having challenged the supposed conceptual differences between the two categories of entitlements, I look at the judiciary, and suggest that social rights and their judicial protection may contribute to our quest for social justice, and that they may promote democracy, rather than undermine it.

Importantly, though, the next part emphasises that we should not focus all our efforts on the judicial enforcement of social rights. The judicial avenue has promise, but it may also be limited, not least because the role of courts is mostly reactive by nature; they get involved only after a violation has occurred and when a case is brought before them. Crucially, the protection of social rights in law is not limited to their judicial protection, and this is a matter that social rights sceptics sometimes disregard. The second aspect of legalisation involves the role of legislators, which this part explores. The argument is that our legislators also have duties to legislate in a manner that will secure access to basic material conditions for the poor and vulnerable. In fact, the legislature has the primary obligation to promote social rights. Legislatures and courts ought to work in partnership for the legal protection of social rights.

The essay then examines the content of social rights, the question of whose duty it is to promote such rights and to whom such duties are owed. It suggests that the endeavour to construe the content of social rights faces different challenges when examining the role of legislatures than when examining the role of courts, and explores some possibilities for rendering the duties concrete. This part then looks at the horizontal application of social rights between private actors.

The sixth part turns to challenges that lay ahead, which, I argue, should form a priority for our legislators and the international community in the process of the legalisation of social rights. It notes two significant shortcomings in relation to the law on social rights, which their opponents perhaps do not always appreciate fully, as they place excessive attention on the justiciability debate. The first problem is the exclusion of foreign nationals who reside unlawfully within a country; the second problem is the neglect of the global poor. Resting on the belief that the legalisation of rights has much to offer in fighting injustices that the poor and vulnerable suffer, this part suggests that the most affluent of us owe duties to foreigners when they are in desperate need, both distant and nearby. Our legislators and the international community ought to address the unequal provision of a minimum level of socio-economic well-being at global level as a matter of priority.

II. A BRIEF, UNHAPPY HISTORY

Social rights are rights to the meeting of basic needs that are essential for human welfare.[2] Although we need to deepen our understanding of the justification for social rights, this definition highlights the point that social rights are entitlements to the avoidance of severe deprivation, not rights to the satisfaction of individual preferences more generally. They incorporate a safeguard against poverty, not the provision of a life in luxury. They are claims of some urgency representing vital interests of the individual to avoid harm. They do not guarantee access to the goods that we each might desire to possess, so as to live a fulfilling life, but they are preconditions for the pursuit of a good life.

In everyday talk, the language of rights is frequently invoked to express a wide variety of claims, which are not always claims to

---

[2] F Michelman, 'On Protecting the Poor through the Fourteenth Amendment' (1969–1970) 83 *Harvard Law Review* 7.

fundamental necessities. This 'rights inflation' has two shortcomings: first, it weakens the moral force and urgency of these claims; second, it leads to conceptions of rights that might not be appropriate for legal (and particularly judicial) protection, which is the focus of the present essay. A narrow definition of social rights can avoid these shortcomings.

Which social rights should our list include? What amounts to a basic need is not self-evident. As a starting point, a list of social rights could be drawn up by reference to legal documents that reflect needs considered basic, mostly, perhaps, in developed industrialised countries. This could contain the following entitlements:

— A right to housing.
— A right to nutrition, including a right to water.
— A right to healthcare.
— A right to education.
— A right to social security and social assistance.
— A right to work and decent working conditions.
— A right to form and join a trade union, including a right to collective bargaining and a right to strike.

The journey towards the recognition and protection of social rights in international law has been slow and tortuous. The international community did not distinguish between civil, political and socio-economic rights in one of its most influential texts, the Universal Declaration of Human Rights (UDHR), adopted under the auspices of the United Nations in the aftermath of the Second World War. The first provisions of the Declaration incorporate rights such as freedom of religion, freedom of expression and the prohibition of torture. From article 22 onwards we find social rights, such as the right to social security, to work, to an adequate standard of living, to rest and leisure, including paid holidays.

That all rights were included in the UDHR is unsurprising to most of us, because the dividing line between civil, political, economic and social rights does not seem to be sharp. Think about freedom of expression, for instance: it can be understood as a civil or a political right, depending on the type of speech we refer to; the right to associate can be classified as political (if it involves political parties), social (if it involves trade unions) or civil (if it refers to organisations of individuals that promote various ideas of the good life). The right to strike can be categorised as social or political, depending on the aim of the strike, and the prohibition of inhuman treatment can be regarded as a civil or a social right, depending on the source of suffering in each case. This also explains why trade union membership belongs to the above list: it serves a dual function of contributing to free political discussion as well as providing protection for jobs and wages.

Although most of us might not be surprised by the inclusion of all groups of rights in the UDHR, Maurice Cranston, one of the staunchest opponents of social rights, said, referring to it: 'What the modern communists have done is to appropriate the word "rights" for the principles that *they* believe in.'[3] Cranston's statement encapsulates well the climate of the Cold War that continues to haunt social rights. The UDHR is not legally enforceable, but it is enormously influential, as it is often referred to in political statements, in human rights campaigns and in the preambles of other legally binding treaties, as well as before courts that pay attention to its content.

Yet the 'modern communists' failed later on. When the international community had to consider whether to make the UDHR legally enforceable, human rights were split between two United Nations Covenants, which were adopted in 1961 and entered into force in 1966: the International Covenant on Civil and Political Rights (ICCPR) and the International Covenant on Economic, Social and Cultural Rights (ICESCR). Rights such as freedom of religion, the right to life and the prohibition of torture were incorporated in the ICCPR. The ICESCR, on the other hand, included rights such as the right to shelter, to healthcare, to fair and just working conditions. In a way that mirrors the separation of human rights into the two UN Covenants, at a regional level

---

[3] M Cranston, *Human Rights To-day* (London, Ampersand, 1962) 38–39.

the Council of Europe and the Organisation of American States separated civil and political rights, and economic and social rights, in two documents: in the former case the European Convention on Human Rights (1950) and in the latter the European Social Charter (1961), and the American Convention on Human Rights (1978)—containing some more extensive socio-economic guarantees than its European counterpart—and the San Salvador Additional Protocol in the Area of Economic, Social and Cultural Rights (1999). Among general regional instruments, the African Charter of Human and Peoples' Rights (1981) opted for the model of the UDHR, and included social rights alongside civil and political rights. In 2000, the European Union adopted the EU Charter of Fundamental Rights that includes civil, political and socio-economic rights. The document was initially non-binding, but now forms part of the Treaty of Lisbon, imposing obligations on the institutions of the European Union and on Member States' authorities when applying or transposing EU law.

The division of human rights in most international human rights treaties was coupled with striking differences in their wording and monitoring. Civil and political rights were drafted in an imperative manner: they could and should be immediately protected. Socio-economic rights appeared in a language that was far less imperative and far more aspirational: they cannot be realised immediately, they require resources and states have discretion as to the steps that they will take to provide them.

The difference in the wording is best illustrated by looking at article 2(1) of each of the Covenants. Article 2(1) of the ICCPR reads as follows:

> Each State Party to the present Covenant undertakes to respect and to ensure to all individuals within its territory and subject to its jurisdiction the rights recognized in the present Covenant, without distinction of any kind, such as race, colour, sex, language, religion, political or other opinion, national or social origin, property, birth or other status.

Article 2(1) of the ICESCR provides:

> Each State Party to the present Covenant undertakes *to take steps*, individually and through international assistance and co-operation, especially economic and technical, *to the maximum of its available resources*, with a view to achieving *progressively* the full realization of the rights recognized in the present Covenant *by all appropriate means*, including particularly the adoption of legislative measures (emphasis added).

The rights of the ICCPR are to be protected immediately, in other words. They are important entitlements that should be guaranteed for everyone. States cannot be indifferent and cannot invoke practicalities to justify their violation. Social rights differ, it seems from article 2(1) of the ICESCR, which makes them conditional on resources, and hence not immediately realisable. An effort should be made, of course, but it is not required that the outcomes be immediately achieved.

The separation of human rights in different treaties led certain countries, like the United States, to ratify only the ICCPR, neglecting the ICESCR. In Europe, at the same time, and as if the separation of human rights in two documents was not an adequate statement of the inferior status that the international community decided to afford to social rights, the drafters of the European Social Charter (ESC) took a step further. They differentiated socio-economic from civil and political rights by opting for a peculiar *a la carte* formulation. States that decided to sign up to this treaty would not have to comply with all its provisions. They could simply choose some of them and ignore the rest.

The division of human rights into two categories should not bother us, unless it has practical consequences. It does. From early on in the history of the United Nations, the ICCPR recognised a right to individual petition before the Human Rights Committee in an additional protocol. Everyone within the contracting states' jurisdiction has a right to bring a complaint for an alleged violation of the Covenant; the Committee examines it and adopts a Communication establishing whether there has been a breach of the ICCPR. The ICESCR, on the other hand, is only monitored through reporting procedures. States undertake an obligation to submit periodic reports to the Committee on Economic Social and Cultural Rights (CESCR) regarding compliance with the ICESCR, which then issues Concluding Observations. It was not until 2008, after lengthy, heated debates, that an optional Protocol on individual petition for violations of social rights came into force. This Protocol that provides for individual petitions for alleged violations of social rights brings the ICESCR and the ICCPR a step closer together.

At regional level, the European and American systems have opted for a model similar to the United Nations. The European Convention on Human Rights (ECHR) provides for a right of individual application before the European Court of Human Rights (ECtHR). The ESC provides a procedure for reporting to the European Committee of Social Rights and, since 1996, a Protocol that recognises a right of collective complaint by certain non-governmental organisations, trade unions and other groups. The American Convention on Human Rights, in a similar vein, is monitored by the Inter-American Court of Human Rights, where individuals can lodge an application for an alleged violation of rights under the Convention, while the San Salvador Protocol in the Area of Economic, Social and Cultural Rights, which was adopted in 1988 and provides for a right to individual petition on the right to education and trade union rights, has not yet entered into force. The EU Charter of Fundamental Rights, incorporated in the Lisbon Treaty, has been approached with scepticism and concern by countries such as the United Kingdom and Poland, which opted out of its socio-economic provisions, even though the Charter only binds institutions of the European Union and not Governments of the Member States except in relation to the application of EU law.

The disparity in the protection of social rights at an international level has been mirrored at a domestic level. The debate over whether social rights should be enforceable through law is in some countries more advanced and more settled than in others. Social rights are a neglected aspect of the US Constitution, which only contains an equality clause that has traditionally been interpreted narrowly by the US Supreme Court as a prohibition of discrimination. The Canadian Charter of Rights and Freedoms only protects civil and political rights in a manner similar to the ECHR. In Europe, the 1998 UK Human Rights Act (HRA) incorporated most rights of the ECHR into domestic law, without incorporating the provisions of the ESC. In several other countries, such as Greece, Spain and Norway, there is a list of socio-economic entitlements in the Constitutions. Yet often in these examples, social rights are not afforded the same status as civil and political rights. They are drafted in weaker terms, and sometimes also included under the heading 'directive principles of policy'. The same can be observed in other jurisdictions such as India, Argentina, Japan and Colombia. There are, finally, few countries where social rights are fully justiciable. South Africa, for instance, saw the incorporation of social rights in its post-apartheid Constitution as having a transformative potential, and included them on the same footing as civil and political rights. Brazil similarly sets out social rights in the Constitution alongside civil and political rights.

The divergence in the constitutional protection afforded to social rights from one country to the other is enormous, but what emerges is that most of the time, even if social rights figure in a legally enforceable document of a higher status than ordinary legislation, they assume a somewhat secondary role to civil and political rights. On the other hand, it can be observed that the academic and political debate about social rights has gained momentum over the last few years in jurisdictions, such as the United Kingdom or the United States, that have been traditionally hostile to the constitutional protection of these claims.

At a domestic level, at the risk of over-simplification and over-generalisation, it can be said that, overall, there is a significant discrepancy in the constitutional protection of social rights when compared to that of civil and political rights. The latter group of entitlements is usually set out in bills of rights, which are sometimes entrenched, meaning that they are given a higher status than ordinary law and can be modified or repealed only through special procedures. The power of state authorities to override our freedom of expression or our right to privacy without being held accountable is limited. As social rights are most often not protected in bills of rights, state action that breaches them is at best susceptible to a lower degree of scrutiny than state action that breaches civil rights. In the few examples, such as South Africa or Brazil, where social rights are set out in the Constitution side by side with civil and political rights, the possibility of asserting them judicially through individual petition exists in a manner similar to civil and political rights. Finally, in countries such as India where social rights are drafted as directive principles of social policy and are expressly stated to be non-justiciable, courts have sometimes examined social rights in the context of claims for breach of justiciable civil and political rights.

Of course, some of the countries that do not protect social rights in their constitutions might grant welfare protection to their citizens through ordinary legislation. Sweden is a good example of a country with a very strong tradition of social legislation. The concern is that in these cases the protection of social rights is vulnerable to change: if social rights are not recognised as abstract principles with a distinct status in national and international law, little can stop a government from repealing such legislation if the economic or social circumstances change (or if otherwise so minded). At the same time, if civil and political rights are constitutionally entrenched while social rights are protected only by ordinary legislation, there is an imbalance in the commitment to a higher level of rights protection, which is hard to justify.

Today, several decades after the end of the Cold War, social rights are still the Cinderella of human rights law.[4] Their weaker protection as compared to civil and political rights is troubling. That the international community and most governments around the world chose to adopt less demanding standards and systems for the protection of socio-economic rights implies that these claims are either different in nature or significance to their civil and political counterparts; that the rights of free expression and

---

[4] Sandra Fredman, *Human Rights Transformed* (Oxford, OUP, 2008).

privacy are weightier or fundamentally different from the rights to shelter, a job, water and food. This cannot be correct.

III. COMMON FOUNDATIONS

The international community and several governments the world over have drawn a sharp line between civil and political rights on the one hand, and socio-economic rights on the other. This carries with it heavy consequences both at a practical level in terms of protection, and at a symbolic level in terms of the commitment to the values that socio-economic provision reflects. A dichotomy that was mostly due to Cold War ideologies, which viewed social rights as communist goals and divided the world in the second half of the twentieth century, came to be entrenched in legally enforceable documents, embracing a wanting conception of the good life in which freedoms of speech and privacy are presented as more valuable than economic well-being. Such conceptualisation of the person in many constitutions and treaties is deficient, because it prioritises some essential conditions of a good life, while neglecting others. The discrepancy in the protection of social rights on the one hand and civil and political rights on the other reflects a troubling failure to capture the vital interests underlying the former, and to mark the urgency of the requirement that they be recognised as principles of a higher status, standards towards which state action should strive and against which it should be assessed.

There are many arguments for the importance of socio-economic rights. Here I will challenge the traditional dichotomy between social rights on the one hand, and civil and political rights on the other by suggesting that the two groups of rights have shared foundations. The neglect of socio-economic rights strikes at the heart of our dignity, liberty and the sense of belonging to our community: the very same values that ground civil and political rights.

A. Dignity

Severe poverty can lead to a variety of adverse predicaments. It might deprive a person of access to medication in case of illness and to food, housing and education. A life in desperate need is a life in which a person lacks the essentials to live in dignity. A person's dignity is respected when others are not permitted to treat her in a degrading and unfair manner. Dignity is also closely connected to the idea of self-respect and the respect of others. The castaway, who is alone on a deserted island, does not suffer a loss of dignity if she has no clothing or food. Yet a desperately needy person that lives in a society where the others are well-off, will probably feel this loss of self-respect and the respect of the others. Dignity is not defined by reference to what a person feels that she should have. It is defined by reference to a person's justified feelings. Someone might feel that it is undignified to fly by plane in economy class, and that it is inconsistent with her dignity not to fly 'business'. Yet this simply reflects the views of a person with a particular background and from a particular social class. It is not a justified feeling shared by everyone.

It is commonly said that dignity is the most appropriate and least controversial basis for human rights because it is something people deserve simply by virtue of being human. For this reason, it is also pronounced in several constitutions and other human rights documents as a basis for civil and political rights. Ill-treatment of people by the police, restrictions on freedom of expression, detention in harsh conditions, are all an affront to dignity. Yet protection of civil and political rights alone does not provide adequate respect for our dignity. Basic material provision is also essential. Dignity lies at the heart of our humanity and grounds the most fundamental elements that are essential for the human condition. Two examples can help us realise the catastrophic effect of poverty on human dignity.

Drinking water when we are thirsty or to get our 1.5 litres of recommended daily intake, basic sanitation or a relaxing foam bath, making a soup when we are hungry, a coffee or tea when we are sleepy or cold, are all activities that many of us take for granted. Lack of water brings thirst, inadequate personal hygiene and illness and may lead to death. Life without water, insofar as someone survives, is an undignified life, because water is a necessary condition for meeting some of the most basic requirements of a decent life. Water is not a luxury, then, unlike a fizzy drink or a beer. It is a basic necessity. For Ms Mazibuko,[5] however, and many others, access to water became a luxury. This occurred when the municipality of Phiri decided to install pre-payment meters in their dwellings, and to stop providing water, unless it had been paid for in advance. This policy was not followed in other richer neighbourhoods of Johannesburg. The effect of the measure was that the inhabitants of Phiri, who were extremely poor and could not afford to pay, lived in appalling conditions.

Going home to rest or to withdraw from public space and act in seclusion is something natural for most of us. We often need to relax and have some time on our own. It is also essential to be able to go to our own place to perform certain activities in private: engaging in some acts (such as sexual intercourse) in public would constitute a criminal offence in many countries. Most of us could probably not envisage life without a home. For Ms Grootboom,[6] however, basic shelter was a luxury. At the beginning of her misfortune she, together with others, lived in shacks in deplorable conditions. They had no water, sewage and refuse removal arrangements, and 95 per cent of them had no electricity. A quarter of the families had no income, and some of them were children. Ms Grootboom, her sister and their families lived in a 20 square-metre shack. The waiting list for state-subsidised housing was many years, so a group of them decided to escape the deplorable conditions and to move onto privately owned vacant land, which had been reserved for cheap housing. The owner obtained an eviction order, but as the squatters had nowhere to go, they remained on the land. In the cold winter of Cape Town, Ms Grootboom and the others were removed from the private land: their shacks were bulldozed and

---

[5] *Mazibuko v City of Johannesburg* (CCT 39/09) 2009 ZACC 28.
[6] *Grootboom v Republic of South Africa* (CCT 11/00) 2000 ZACC 19.

burnt; their belongings were destroyed. They moved again, this time to a sports field, and filed an application for shelter with the municipality and then the court in South Africa.

Ms Mazibuko and Ms Grootboom are examples of people who live in desperation as a result of a lack of access to basic necessities, such as water and shelter. Their appalling conditions deeply affect their ability to pursue worthwhile goals; they also have an impact on their sense of self-respect and the respect of the others that are at the heart of the notion of human dignity. These examples remind us that basic social rights are as central to dignity as civil and political rights. There are two further values that can shed light on the shared foundations of socio-economic and civil and political rights: liberty and citizenship.

B. Liberty

Liberty is a cherished value, and for many it grounds only civil rights. Arbitrary detention, restriction of the right to express ourselves or infringement of our privacy seem incongruent with the belief in liberty, and the primacy often afforded to the protection of civil and political rights in international human rights law and in national legal systems partly expresses this. When it comes to economic need, people are reluctant to present it as lack of liberty. In the best case, it is presented as lack of *ability* to pursue certain activities because of scarce resources.

When thinking of the individual in relation to the state, liberty is usually seen as imposing restraints on governmental power. We have a right to life, religion, expression—these are our liberties—and the correlative duty of the authorities is to abstain from interference with these liberties. The poor and needy are certainly unfortunate. Yet their plight does not constitute a violation of their liberty, some think. Though they may have other grounds to complain, such as equality or justice, they cannot be said to be unfree. Insofar as the government does not act, insofar as it does not take positive steps to interfere with certain liberties, it cannot be blamed for making us unfree, so the libertarian argument goes. Libertarianism only recognises negative duties of the state not to interfere with civil liberties.

Yet, saying that liberty grounds civil rights only is flawed. There is a different, more appealing approach to liberty, which leads to a richer understanding of state duties. This was captured by Roosevelt in his proclamation that 'true individual freedom cannot exist without economic security and independence. Necessitous men are not free men'.[7] It was also expressed with passion by one of the delegates during the drafting of the ECHR: 'What indeed does freedom mean?' it was asked, '[w]hat does the inviolability of the home mean for the man who has got no home? What is the value of sacred family rights and family liberties for the father who is permanently haunted by the spectre of unemployment?'[8]

Liberty and resources are inextricably linked, because our rules that regulate property impose normative constraints on the liberty of others. The impact of economic need on freedom was analysed by GA Cohen in his essay 'Freedom and Money',[9] which argued that lack of money restricts not only our ability to act but also our freedom. An example that Cohen uses to illustrate the links between freedom and resources is that of a woman who wants to go to Glasgow to visit her family, but has no money to pay her train fare. To the statement that she is still free to travel, we would respond that this understanding of freedom is too narrow, because as soon as this woman gets on a train without a ticket, she will be asked to get off.

The plight of homelessness, to give another example, involves the restriction of numerous freedoms. A person who attempts to find shelter in someone's property will be asked to leave. The freedom of the homeless to act is too limited, because in order to be free to do something, as Waldron put it, we need to be able to

[7] FD Roosevelt, Address Before the Democratic National Convention, 1936.

[8] European Convention on Human Rights, *Travaux Préparatoires* (Leiden, Martinus Nijhoff, 1985) vol I, 42.

[9] GA Cohen, 'Freedom and Money' available at www.howardism.org/appendix/Cohen.pdf

do it somewhere.[10] The homeless person, however, has nowhere to go, other than sleep rough in the street. How can we say that people are free, then, if the options that are open to them are extremely limited (if they have any at all) because of the constraints that our property rules impose? People are not free if they do not have at least some valuable choices; people are completely unfree if they have no choice at all. Given that societies are organised by some form of market economy, in which someone's liberty is restricted by others' legal rights, choice and resources are inextricably linked. We cannot have liberty without basic resources. We cannot be free without some basic social rights.

Negative and positive aspects of liberty, moreover, are closely intertwined. This is evident when thinking about the relationship between civil and political rights on the one hand, and socio-economic rights on the other. As explained earlier, the international community and most national governments accepted without much hesitation that civil and political rights should be legally protected and enforceable through courts, unlike their socio-economic counterparts. These rights, which are otherwise called 'civil *liberties*' in some jurisdictions, have traditionally been regarded as rights to important freedoms, such as expression or religion, from the sphere of which the state should abstain. If state authorities interfere with liberty without proper justification and in a disproportionate manner, civil liberties are violated. While civil and political rights are seen in some legal cultures as rights to freedom, social rights are traditionally presented as rights to state provision rather than abstention. Housing, work and education are entitlements that require that the authorities act and allocate resources for the provision of these social goods, imposing positive duties.

Yet, it slowly emerged that the division between civil liberties and socio-economic rights is far from sharp. Negative and positive liberties may lend support to each other. In 1993, for instance, the World Conference on Human Rights adopted the

---

[10] J Waldron, 'Homelessness and the Issue of Freedom' in *Liberal Rights* (Cambridge, CUP, 1993) 309.

Vienna Declaration and Programme for Action which stated that 'all human rights are universal, indivisible, interdependent and interrelated. The international community must treat human rights globally in a fair and equal manner, on the same footing, and with the same emphasis.'[11] Numerous declarations of the international community repeated that all human rights are closely linked, and this same position was advanced in the preambles of several treaties. Some examples help to illustrate how rights can be interdependent. The right to vote is probably meaningless for someone who is uneducated and uninformed. The good we have in mind when recognising the right involves more than the physical liberty of ticking a box. Unless individuals are in a position to understand the options in front of them, this freedom to cast a vote is trivial. Is this person free to vote? The right to privacy has little substance for someone who has no shelter and can never withdraw to act in seclusion. Does this person enjoy private life? Rights to the traditional and widely endorsed liberties are often rendered vacuous rhetoric, without a level of social provision. A certain degree of basic socio-economic provision is a prerequisite for the effective exercise of civil and political freedoms.

The truth is that the plight of destitution can be seen as affecting many aspects of liberty: the liberty to act, the liberty to pursue happiness and even the liberty to think, for someone who lacks basic material conditions is gravely concerned with survival and does not have the luxury to think about much other than that. Liberty is not a foundation of civil and political rights only, but of social rights too. The only sense in which the desperately destitute person is free is that whatever she does, she has not much to lose. However, this cannot be what we have in mind when we refer to the sanctity of liberty!

[11] Vienna Declaration and Programme for Action (12 July 1993) A/CONF.157/23 para 5.

C. Citizenship: Rights and Belonging

It is an affront to our dignity to have no access to the essential minima for subsistence. The notion of freedom is empty rhetoric if it is simply defined as a freedom to barely exist, without also encompassing the possibility to think and to act in any meaningful way. Yet, social rights are not only essential for the dignity and freedom of the person. They are also essential for community membership. The relationship between individual rights and belonging to a community is best captured by the idea of citizenship.

Citizenship bridges the gap between liberalism that places its main attention on the value of the person, and communitarianism that focuses on the importance of the community. The *locus classicus* on rights of citizenship is the theory of the British sociologist TH Marshall. In his influential essay, 'Citizenship and Social Class', Marshall defined citizenship as 'a status bestowed on those who are full members of a community. All who possess the status are equal with respect to the rights and duties with which the status is endowed.'[12] Crucially, equal community membership has come to enshrine a wealth of rights. It has three elements: the civil, the political and the social.

> The civil element is composed of the rights necessary for individual freedom—liberty of the person, freedom of speech, thought and faith, the right to own property and to conclude valid contracts, and the right to justice. [. . .] By the political element, I mean the right to participate in the exercise of political power, as a member of a body invested with political authority or as an elector of the members of such a body. [. . .] By the social element, I mean the whole range from the right to a modicum of economic welfare and security to the right to share to the full in the social heritage and to live the life of a civilized being according to the standards prevailing in the society.[13]

---

[12] TH Marshall, 'Citizenship and Social Class' in R Goodin and P Pettit (eds), *Contemporary Political Philosophy—An Anthology* (Cambridge, Blackwell, 1997) 291 at 300. The essay was originally published in 1949.
[13] ibid 294.

Citizenship includes a social element, which is not a matter of charity with the stigma attached to it that distinguishes between citizens and poor outsiders. A basic level of material conditions is a matter of right and the state ought to secure it as such, with equal respect for everyone. It is essential for community membership, as much as civil and political rights are, without which one is excluded and isolated. The idea of citizenship suggests, first, that stability requires treating the members of the community with equal respect and, second, that social rights are an essential element of membership. Citizenship enriches our analysis by focusing on the role of membership in society, while accepting the importance of the person's individuality through the recognition of rights.

Citizenship is not a synonym for nationality in this context. Like equality, for example, it is a normative concept both as regards the rights that are attached to it and the persons that it encompasses.[14] It means that everyone should be the beneficiary of *all* groups of rights. To neglect social rights is to exclude people from membership. Those who are excluded from membership will be isolated. They might even seek to subvert the society that does not treat them as members. It also means that *everyone* should be the subject of these rights. It entails a universalist ideal. The aim of the inclusive society is to treat all persons as equal members; the restriction of basic social rights on the grounds of nationality should require special justification. Social rights should not be foreclosed, for instance, at least to those that are permanent residents, employed and taxed in a country, who contribute to the system as much as nationals do.

Like civil and political rights, social rights are essential for dignity, liberty and citizenship; they are crucial for the person both as a member of a state and against state authorities if they treat the person with disrespect. They have shared foundations with civil and political rights and are as crucial as civil and political rights are. Moreover, something significant is gained by thinking about access to fundamental necessities in terms of moral rights.

---

[14] J Waldron, 'Social Citizenship and the Defence of Welfare Provision' in *Liberal Rights* (Cambridge, CUP, 1993) 271.

The role of using the language of entitlements is evident, if we express the same claim in a different vocabulary. The sentence 'I have a right to housing' entails a moral imperative that cannot be captured by the sentences 'I would prefer not to be homeless' or 'It would be good if I had a home', or even 'I need shelter'. Having basic social *rights* invests these claims with normative weight, and necessarily implies that others have a duty to respect, protect and fulfil these rights. Such is the weight and urgency of these claims that any decent government must prioritise them. Is it justified, then, that so many constitutional traditions and the international community too, decided to treat social rights as subordinate?

IV. LEGALISATION

Even though social rights are grounded on the same values as civil and political rights, many countries and international organisations maintain what Keith Ewing described as an 'unbalanced Constitution'.[15] They place their focus on civil liberties and neglect questions of suffering stemming from material deprivation. This situation is problematic and it misses the point that the best expression of the importance given to moral rights by a state is through their protection in law, through their legalisation. Importantly, it needs to be added, it is not sufficient to protect social rights in ordinary legislation, which could be easily repealed by successive governments.

Like civil and political rights, rights to the satisfaction of basic needs should be constitutionalised or otherwise given a distinct status than ordinary legislation. They should be drafted as abstract principles reflecting the aims of decent government and setting limits to its powers. Constitutional rights, particularly when entrenched, can only be repealed through special procedures; hence, they take on the priority that they deserve. At a practical level,

---

[15] K Ewing, 'The Unbalanced Constitution' in T Campbell, K Ewing, A Tomkins (eds), *Sceptical Essays on Human Rights* (Oxford, OUP, 2001) 103.

the constitutionalisation of social rights requires that all legislation and administrative action be compatible with them. At a symbolic level, affording a high status to the rights to the satisfaction of basic needs recognises that decent material conditions are an aim of high priority, an ideal towards which government aspires and a measure against which its actions are assessed. It also shows that social rights have equal weight to civil and political rights, which liberal states have traditionally protected in constitutions.

It is sometimes suggested that it is a bad idea to legalise rights, for the reason that claims of social justice should be left to the political arena; that the legal protection of 'social rights' depoliticises people, as if these words have a magic power that can affect the interest in politics. The statement that rights depoliticise is correct only in the sense that rights are above politics and should not be decided in ordinary political discourse. Social rights, like civil and political rights, have a high priority and ought to be removed from political bargaining. They have to be protected irrespective of whether we have a socialist or a conservative government. Social rights 'trump'[16] the utilitarian calculations of markets, which promote economic efficiency only. They provide a safety net that ensures that no one will suffer overwhelmingly by the failures of our economic or social system, no matter what the government prefers. In this sense, rights to basic goods *ought to* be above politics. Their legalisation and particularly their constitutional protection, serves this purpose by sheltering them from everyday political bargaining.

At the same time, the statement that social rights in constitutions depoliticise people is deeply misleading. Constitutional social rights embody a profound political statement that the provision of basic material conditions is not a matter of charity, but a matter of individual entitlement on the part of the needy which imposes duties on the affluent. The concern of the opponents of the 'social rights discourse' is mistaken because social rights in fact

---

[16] I am borrowing the term 'rights as trumps' from Ronald Dworkin, who uses it to refer to civil rights. See R Dworkin, 'Rights as Trumps' in J Waldron (ed), *Theories of Rights* (Oxford, OUP, 1984) 153.

have the potential to inspire political movements rather than lead to apathy, to motivate individuals and encourage them to engage with questions that they might otherwise only see as an optional matter, rather than an urgent political duty. In this sense, social rights can mobilise and *politicise* people profoundly.

How has the unequal attention to social rights, as opposed to civil and political rights, been justified? Can this justification stand up to scrutiny?

A. Conceptual Differences

The discrepancy between the legal protection of civil and political rights on the one hand and rights to basic material conditions on the other was in the past explained by reasons that appear formalistic, although we can probably identify their normative underpinnings. On a view that prevailed in the second half of the twentieth century, but has some supporters even today, there is a sharp conceptual division between civil and social rights, which makes the latter group inappropriate for legalisation. The real reason that inspired this scepticism was the question of whether social rights should be constitutionalised and made justiciable through courts.

On one view, social rights are conceptually different to civil and political rights in three respects: first, they are positive and require government action; second, they are costly, demanding state expenditure; third, they are abstract. All these characteristics supposedly bring them into sharp contrast with civil and political rights, which are said to be negative, cost-free and concrete.

Several examples can be used to demonstrate that the separation between the two groups of rights is not so sharp: having a right to a fair trial requires an independent judiciary, which can be expensive to maintain (a civil right that is costly); the right to housing might simply require state authorities to stay a person's eviction from her home (a social right that is cost-free); the prohibition of torture demands a well-trained police force that will not take advantage of its position of power to abuse individuals (a civil right that requires state action); the right to work might impose an obligation to refrain from dismissing people for unfair reasons (a social right that requires abstention); fair elections demand setting up polling centres and a machinery to supervise the procedure (a political right that is costly and positive). The sections that follow show that the claim that the two categories of rights differ conceptually is exaggerated and fails after closer inspection.

1. Positive rights

It is often suggested that social rights are positive and require government action and provision of goods, while civil and political rights are negative requiring government abstention. This point is questionable, because both groups of rights can be grounded on liberty, as I showed earlier, and they can all impose both positive and negative duties. Rights are not in themselves positive or negative. In some jurisdictions, like the United States, this point is missed by courts, which insist that constitutional rights only impose negative duties. In the case *Deshaney v Winnebago County Social Services Department*,[17] for instance, the Supreme Court held that no constitutional duty was breached by the authorities' failure to protect a mentally challenged boy who was badly abused by his father. Yet, other jurisdictions provide ample recognition of positive duties that human rights law can impose, showing that civil rights can be positive. In Europe, in *Oneryildiz v Turkey*,[18] the ECtHR examined whether Turkish authorities violated the right to life by not taking the necessary measures to protect the applicants' relatives, who used to live in extremely poor conditions in a site used as a rubbish tip. Following an explosion and a landslide that engulfed some slum dwellings, 39 people died. The Court held that Turkey violated the right to life by not having taken the necessary positive action to protect human life. The fact that the area was dangerous and that the authorities knew or ought to have known of the danger, constituted particularly weighty considerations in the reasoning.

[17] *Deshaney v Winnebago County Social Services Department*, 489 US 189 (1989).
[18] *Oneryildiz v Turkey* App No 48939/99 (Judgment of 30 November 2004).

Social rights are not always positive; they also give rise to negative duties. This has been exemplified in case law from South Africa and the ICESCR. The right to housing might impose a duty to stay evictions, as the South African Constitutional Court held in *Grootboom v Republic of South Africa*[19] and in *Port Elizabeth Municipality v Various Occupiers.*[20] Similarly, when the CESCR found a country to be in violation of the ICESCR for the first time, the finding related to the right to housing and concerned massive expulsions of about 15,000 families in the Dominican Republic.[21] In another case it emphasised that 'evictions carried out in this way not only infringe upon the right to adequate housing but also on the inhabitants' rights to privacy and security of the home'.[22] The CESCR has often thereafter examined forced evictions and restated in its General Comment No 4 on the right to housing, which provides authoritative interpretation of the ICESCR, that forced evictions may constitute a violation of the Covenant.

In order to rebut the positive/negative division between different groups of rights, Henry Shue argued that what is negative or positive is not the right itself, but the duties that correspond to it. He said that duties that are correlative to rights are threefold: 'i. Duties to avoid depriving. ii. Duties to protect from deprivation. iii. Duties to aid the deprived'.[23] The positive/negative rights dichotomy is misconceived on this analysis too, for each right might impose several different duties that can be positive or negative, so it is incorrect to suggest that social rights necessarily impose positive duties, while civil rights are always negative.

2. Costs

Sometimes the satisfaction of rights to basic material conditions requires public spending; a matter that leads to conflicts when there is scarcity of resources. However, the above examples of

---

[19] *Grootboom* (n 6).
[20] *Port Elizabeth Municipality v Various Occupiers* (CCT 53/03) 2004 ZACC 7.
[21] Dominican Republic, ICESCR, E/1991/23 (1990) 55 at para. 249.
[22] Panama, ICESCR, E/1992/23 (1991) 24 at para. 135.
[23] H Shue, *Basic Rights*, 2nd edn (Princeton, Princeton University Press, 1996) 52.

forced evictions show that aspects of social rights, such as the right to housing, might not impose costly duties on state authorities. On the other hand, civil and political rights may have significant resource implications, as the example of *Oneryildiz* reminds us. In a number of cases against Ukraine,[24] moreover, the ECtHR had to examine the compatibility with the ECHR of extremely poor prison conditions. The Court said that the country's limited resources cannot justify prison conditions that attain the minimum level of severity contrary to the prohibition of torture, inhuman and degrading treatment. Human treatment, which is an absolute right, can sometimes demand significant public spending.

At the same time, socio-economic questions with resource implications do not necessarily appear in the guise of constitutional social or human rights claims. They also arise in the process of judicial review of administrative action. In the United Kingdom, the judiciary was in the past reluctant to decide such matters when they were likely to have wide resource implications, holding that the relevant resource-demanding questions are not for courts to decide. This was exemplified in a case involving access to medical treatment for a 10-year-old child that suffered from acute leukaemia. In the opinion of Sir Thomas Bingham MR,

> [d]ifficult and agonising judgments have to be made as to how a limited budget is best allocated to the maximum advantage of the maximum number of patients. That is not a judgment which the court can make. In my judgment, it is not something that a health authority such as this authority can be fairly criticized for not advancing before the court.[25]

Later on, however, Anne Marie Rogers won a legal battle involving Herceptin, a drug that treats breast cancer.[26] She based her application for judicial review of the decision not to provide the drug on the 1977 National Health Service Act, and claimed

---

[24] See, for instance, *Khokhlich v Ukraine* App No 41707/98 (Judgment of 29 April 2003) para 181.

[25] *R v Cambridge Health Authority, ex p B* [1995] 2 All ER 129 (CA).

[26] *The Queen on the application of Ann Marie Rogers v Swindon NHS Primary Care Trust* [2006] EWCA Civ 392 (CA) (Civ Div).

that the refusal of the authorities to provide her and others in her condition access to the drug that would significantly prolong her life was unlawful. This was because Herceptin, an unlicensed drug, was made available in an unprincipled manner. While certain local authorities funded the drug on the basis of clinical recommendation, others provided it if the applicant had an exceptional need. The Court of Appeal ruled that this policy was unlawful. The demand on a pool of potentially eligible women that they demonstrate 'personal circumstances' over and above other women in that pool was irrational.

Questions about the lawfulness of allocating resources are not unique to the constitutionalisation of social rights. Courts already address this kind of question in civil and political rights claims that sometimes have significant budgetary implications, but also in the context of administrative law, when looking at the lawfulness of executive action.

3. *Vagueness*

The content of social rights, finally, is not bound to be abstract. Social rights might appear to be abstract, because they have been neglected in legal scholarship, and until recently the effort to explore their meaning has not been as systematic as the analysis of civil and political rights. For instance, nothing in the ECHR tells us whether extradition to a country where someone is likely to face the death row phenomenon prior to the death penalty, violates the prohibition of inhuman treatment.[27] Nor does the Convention explicitly provide for the right of transsexuals not to disclose their sex to the authorities as an aspect of their private life.[28]

Yet today in Europe people take it for granted that human rights law imposes these duties. The reason why it is taken for granted is not because the provisions are clearly applicable in these

[27] On this see, amongst others, *Soering v UK* App No 14038/88 (Judgment of 7 July 1989).
[28] *Sheffield and Horsham v UK* App Nos 22885/93 and 23390/94 (Judgment of 30 July 1998).

situations. It is rather the other way round. It is through moral argument, extensive academic debate, legal advocacy, and judicial interpretation that the scope of civil and political rights appears to be relatively clear and precise, constantly illuminated and further enriched.ᵃFor the opposite reason, because of lack of rigorous engagement with their content by courts, practitioners, academic scholars and others, socio-economic rights are underexplored and appear to lack precision. Engagement with the content of these rights cannot guarantee that their meaning will be elucidated immediately. Yet it guarantees that a debate will begin, which is the only way in which we can advance our understanding of social rights and deepen our analysis of the duties to which they give rise.

4. The 'Integrated Approach'

Additional evidence that the line between civil and social rights is blurred emerged when courts in several jurisdictions began to recognise that a state act that violates a social right can in fact breach a treaty or a constitution that protects civil and political rights. In a development that marked a significant breakthrough in our understanding of the links between social and civil and political rights, some courts started to accept that both groups of rights have similar moral weight, and they are sometimes so closely intertwined that a breach of a social right can constitute a violation of a civil or political right. In this way, they made social rights indirectly effective in jurisdictions that do not grant them direct legal effect. The ECtHR case of *Sidabras and Dziautas v Lithuania*[29] exemplifies this trend. In this case the applicants were dismissed and banned from access to public and private sector employment for a period of 10 years because of their status as former agents of the KGB. The Court was prepared to accept that the right to private life, protected under article 8 of the ECHR, can encompass what was in substance the applicants' right to work. The case is, therefore, a paradigm example of an interpretive method that has

[29] *Sidabras and Dziautas v Lithuania* App Nos 55480/00 and 59330/00 (Judgment of 27 July 2004).

come to be known as an 'integrated approach'[30] to the interpretation of civil and political rights instruments, which opens them up to claims of economic deprivation.

A similar position has been adopted in several other jurisdictions, such as Israel, Canada, Namibia, Ireland and Spain, where social rights are not directly justiciable. In the United Kingdom, perhaps the best illustration of the interpretive method that reads socio-economic entitlements into civil and political rights documents is the *R (on the application of Limbuela, Tesema and Adam) v Secretary of State for the Home Department* case,[31] mentioned in the introduction of this essay. The applicants, destitute asylum seekers, challenged the compatibility with the prohibition of inhuman and degrading treatment of the withdrawal of state support that resulted in extreme hardship. In an important judgment, the House of Lords held that the extremity of the circumstances reached the minimum level of severity of treatment required for the provision to be applicable. They held that extreme socio-economic deprivation in this case constituted a breach of the ECHR.

Special mention ought to be made of India when examining the trend that views civil and social rights as closely linked. The Supreme Court of India regularly reads socio-economic rights into the list of civil rights that the Constitution enshrines. Although social rights are only recognised as non-enforceable principles of social policy in the document, the Court has frequently held that the constitutionally protected right to life demands a certain degree of socio-economic provision. In *Olga Tellis v Bombay Municipal Corporation*,[32] for instance, it stated that the right to life that is protected under article 21 of the Constitution includes a right to livelihood.

The adoption of the integrated approach to the interpretation of civil and political rights shows that even in countries that do not

---

[30] V Mantouvalou, 'Work and Private Life: Sidabras and Dziautas v Lithuania' (2005) 30 *European Law Review* 573.

[31] *R (on the application of Limbuela, Tesema and Adam) v Secretary of State for the Home Department* [2005] UKHL 66.

[32] *Olga Tellis v Bombay Municipal Corporation*, Supreme Court of India, 1985, AIR 1986 Supreme Court 18.

explicitly recognise social rights in their constitutions, these might sometimes impose similar requirements to, or indeed amount to essential preconditions to the enjoyment of, the more traditional civil liberties. What is important to realise is that the supposed conceptual differences between the two categories collapses when advocates, courts and scholars engage in a substantive examination of their moral weight. All entitlements have similarities and can lend support to each other.

The claim that there is a sharp analytical division between civil, political, economic and social rights is overly formalistic. This debate is really a distorted reflection of certain judgments about the limits of adjudication, which lies in the heart of the debate on social rights. The problem is that many social rights sceptics are in fact sceptics of judicial review. They do not dislike social rights as such; they just oppose a particular form of their protection. The trouble with this approach, though, is that by rejecting justiciability, they reject legalisation of social rights altogether. This position is flawed, as will be demonstrated in the sections that follow.

B. The Role of Courts

Contradictory
↳ Massive
Cost

What is the role of courts in the protection of social rights? The answer to this question is twofold. First, the judiciary serves a crucial accountability function. Second, it provides an avenue for the poor and vulnerable to have their voice heard, which political fora do not always secure.

It was suggested earlier that rights to the satisfaction of basic needs are weighty moral considerations, and that the best way to show that we are serious about our commitment to these claims is by protecting them in law. Legalisation would mean little, however, if we had no mechanism by which to hold the perpetrators of injustices to account. The government is held to account in elections, of course. By voting, we express our endorsement of, or dissatisfaction with, its policies. Yet in elections the decisions of the majorities always prevail. The voice of dissatisfied minorities, vulnerable groups and individuals that are oppressed and treated unjustly, is often too weak to be heard. When state authorities run amok, when the legislature and executive pursue the interests of majorities or powerful elites, we need to be able to question them and hold them accountable. The best way to hold them accountable is through an independent body that will scrutinise their actions and will require them to give reasons for their decisions. At the same time, courts offer an avenue for the weak and vulnerable to be heard that democratic politics might not necessarily provide. By having their voice heard, the poor and excluded attract attention that they might otherwise not get.

The justiciability sceptics, who are often well-meaning scholars that believe in social justice, voice concerns about the role of judges in the protection of social rights. Some of these concerns are more justified than others, yet none of these justifies the rejection of justiciability altogether. First, they say that the judiciary does not have the necessary expertise to examine the compatibility of legislative and administrative action with social rights. Second, they argue that judges are hostile towards social rights. Third, they claim that courts have no legitimacy to examine complaints against the legislative and executive branches of government. By voicing these concerns, they reject social rights litigation without realising its full potential. Even more worryingly, they reject constitutionalisation as such, as if constitutional litigation is all that the legal protection of social rights is about. More will be said on this later.

1. Expertise

A matter that is commonly presented as lying in the heart of the adjudication of social rights is the question of courts' expertise, which some say is lacking. Social rights are supposed to raise questions of a technical nature, which should be left to housing experts, economists and healthcare providers to address. However, as Alston has perceptively stated,

> [t]o suggest that economic rights issues should be dealt with exclusively by economists and others is tantamount to suggesting

that civil and political rights issues should be seen as the exclusive domain of criminologists, trade unionists, psychologists, physicians, pediatricians, the clergy, communication experts and others.[33]

However, human rights *law* itself is an area of expertise. In addition, even if the court lacks technical knowledge, judges can be trained and can hear experts' opinions, as frequently happens in court. It is also important to remember that courts already adjudicate on claims to socio-economic provision in the context of judicial review of administrative action. Here, courts often assess technical socio-economic questions of healthcare or tax legislation, for instance, in order to examine if state authorities have acted lawfully.

In the same way that experts participate in a criminal trial to assess forensic evidence, they could also take part in a case that involves the right to healthcare, for instance, in order to assess medical issues that reach beyond the court's knowledge. In addition, the judiciary could also take note of materials produced by expert bodies that have previously examined the matters under consideration, something that already happens in certain jurisdictions. On a technical matter of healthcare, the courts could consider relevant materials of the World Health Organisation, and on a labour-related matter, materials of the International Labour Organisation (ILO).

Judges already hear social rights claims in applying ordinary legislation. They can also be trained to deal with technical socio-economic questions, and can take note of experts' opinions when such questions arise. Can we trust that they will properly protect social rights, though, or is the attitude of the judiciary such as to make this endeavour hopeless?

2. *Judicial attitudes towards the claims of the needy*

The second concern of justiciability sceptics is that judges are hostile to social rights claims, and should not be entrusted with

---

[33] P Alston, 'US Ratification of the Covenant on Economic, Social and Cultural Rights: The Need for an Entirely New Strategy' (1990) 84 *American Journal of International Law* 365, 375.

this task. In some jurisdictions, there are examples from the case law that justify the scepticism about affording courts the power to adjudicate on social rights. In the United Kingdom, for instance, courts are notoriously reluctant to protect such claims—a point that is exemplified in numerous labour law cases. In the United States, it is established jurisprudence that constitutional rights do not impose positive obligations, and it is unlikely that the courts will easily change their position.

Yet, even if courts are sometimes hostile to social rights, they are not always so. This was evident, for instance, in the House of Lords judgment in the *Limbuela* case that was discussed in the introduction of this essay. Other jurisdictions where courts have been open to social rights claims include the Council of Europe, where the ECtHR has issued important decisions in recent years, such as the *Sidabras and Džiautas* case mentioned earlier that marked a reversal of the jurisprudence that excluded social concerns from the scope of the Convention. This case has been followed by a line of important decisions protecting socio-economic interests in the ECHR. The case *Demir and Baykara v Turkey*[34] of the Grand Chamber of the ECtHR, which concerns collective labour rights, contains detailed analysis on the importance of social rights materials for the interpretation of the Convention.

Furthermore, evidence from research conducted in new democracies and developing countries shows that the judiciary has potential to play, and sometimes has indeed played a role in social transformation. Several examples from jurisdictions in Latin America, Eastern Europe, Africa and Asia exhibit its potential, which has been described by Gargarella, Domingo and Roux as 'an institutional voice for the poor'.[35] To this interesting comparative study that presents the role of courts in social change, it is crucial to add an important collection of empirical studies on the role of social rights adjudication in developing countries. The study

[34] *Demir and Baykara v Turkey* App No 34503/97 (Judgment of 12 November 2008).

[35] R Gargarella, P Domingo and T Roux (eds), *Courts and Social Transformation in New Democracies* (Aldershot, Ashgate, 2006).

'Courting Social Justice'[36] gathers and analyses evidence on the role of courts in the making of social policy. Gauri and Brinks find that in countries such as India, Brazil and Indonesia, courts are neither excessively activist nor unduly deferential. In the case studies, judges are revealed to be open to the claims of the needy, a fact that is largely attributed to the process of appointments of judges in these countries. Their decisions, in turn, 'do not so much stop or hijack the policy debate as inject the language of rights into it and add another forum for debate'.[37] The evidence emerging from developing countries and new democracies does not imply that their particular model of social rights protection and judicial appointments should serve as a paradigm for developed countries or old democracies. It suggests, however, that the judiciary can be open to claims for social justice and even drive social change in certain circumstances, a point that is often neglected by justiciability sceptics.

There are further important examples of individual judges who have exhibited responsiveness to the claims of the needy. Judge Albie Sachs of the Constitutional Court of South Africa is one of the most enlightened and inspiring instances. Judge Sachs has sat in important social rights cases and has also published extensively on the role of social rights in courts. In the autobiographical book *The Strange Alchemy of Life and Law*, Sachs described the painful process of adjudicating socio-economic rights. Sachs's sensitivity to the claims of the weak and the economically vulnerable is particularly evident in Chapter 7, entitled 'The Judge who Cried: The Judicial Enforcement of Socio-Economic Rights', where he makes reference to the *Hoffman* case involving the refusal of South African Airways to hire an HIV-positive individual.[38] Delivering a judgment that upheld Mr Hoffman's right to be employed by South African Airways, Judge Sachs describes how his eyes were

---

[36] V Gauri, DM Brinks (eds), *Courting Social Justice* (Cambridge, CUP, 2008).

[37] V Gauri and DM Brinks, 'A New Policy Landscape: Legalizing Social and Economic Rights in the Developing World' in Gauri and Brinks, *Courting Social Justice* (2008) 303 at 304 and 343.

[38] *Hoffman v South African Airways* (Case CCT 17/00) 2000 ZACC 17 (Constitutional Court of South Africa).

filled with tears, feeling 'an overwhelming sense of pride at being a member of a court that protected fundamental rights and secured dignity for all'.[39]

The hostile attitude of the judiciary towards socio-economic claims of the needy in certain countries might be explained by the background and training of judges. In the United Kingdom for instance, it is commonly said that most senior judges are middle or upper-class, white males, educated at elitist institutions. However, if it is proven that courts have a negative attitude towards social rights, and that this is due to the lack of judicial diversity, the best response is to create a diverse judiciary, rather than give up on judicial enforcement. For the loss that we will suffer if we give up on judicial enforcement altogether—the lack of accountability for injustices suffered by the weakest amongst us with which we will be faced, the uncontrolled exercise of executive and legislative power—will cost us much more than the effort that we need to put in rethinking the training and appointments of our judges. For this reason, concerns over the character of the judiciary should be addressed by revising the appointment methods and by training the judges according to the requirements of their role, rather than abandoning the idea of the judicial protection of social rights altogether.

The empirical claim that judges may be hostile to socio-economic interests cannot take us far in our normative enquiry. Although these are valid concerns in certain jurisdictions, the action that is needed is not to abandon justiciable social rights altogether, for the cost would be too high for our societies to bear. What is needed is reform of judicial appointment processes and training of the judiciary.

3. Legitimacy

Let us now turn to the legitimacy objection. A central constitutional principle of the modern state is that of the separation of the

---

[39] A Sachs, *The Strange Alchemy of Life and Law* (Oxford, OUP, 2009) 183.

legislative, executive and judicial power. If social rights are made justiciable, the judiciary may sometimes be involved in resource allocation, which is said to be the exclusive area of the elected government. Would this violate the doctrine of the separation of powers?

The judicial protection of social rights is not a breach of the principle of the separation of powers. First, there is no sharp analytical division between social rights and civil and political rights, a point shown earlier. This necessarily means that if social rights, or better some of their correlative duties, bear close resemblance to civil and political rights, then the legitimacy objection should apply equally to all human rights claims, at least when they give rise to duties that are costly or positive. It would imply that when the right to a fair trial imposes a duty to train judges, or when the right not to be tortured imposes a duty to train the police force, courts should not have the power to decide these cases, so as to not interfere with the government's budget. Yet because all rights can be costly, wouldn't this view of the role of courts in their protection be dangerously narrow?

To the contrary, the judicial protection of social rights upholds the principle of the separation of powers. This is because the idea of the separation of powers does not require a watertight division between the legislative, the executive and the judicial branches of government. It is, instead, tied to the idea of 'checks and balances', which means that each of the branches of government ought to supervise the others, so as to ensure that they do not abuse their allocated powers. The real question, then, involves the extent of acceptable supervision, rather than whether there will be any supervision at all. We need courts to scrutinise the acts of the executive and legislative branches, but we might not want them to design the budget. This can be achieved through the appropriate type of judicial review of legislative and administrative action (that will be discussed later on), rather than the rejection of justiciability as such.

The issue of institutional competence should not be seen as giving rise to 'all or nothing' solutions. The real reason why some people invoke the separation of powers as an argument against justiciability is because they believe that democracy is compromised by allowing judges to reach decisions on resource allocation. This view brings democracy to the forefront of the justiciability debate.

4. *Democracy*

If we rejected the justiciability of social rights as undemocratic, as some sceptics do, we would lose sight of the fact that democracy, properly understood, requires satisfaction of certain basic needs. Crucially, also, the judicial protection of social rights corrects some of the deficiencies of our democratic systems.

Let us, first, consider the key definitions. Social rights are rights to the satisfaction of basic needs. Democracy is a contested concept. One of its fundamental principles is that people participate in the creation of the rules by which they are governed. When reference is made to this system of governance, we do not usually have in mind direct democracy. Democracy is today indirect and representative. Decisions reached are rarely unanimous; they are made by majorities. To suggest that any decision reached by a majority is democratic, though, would reflect a poor and inadequate view of democracy. There is a richer conception of democracy, liberal democracy, which contains other fundamental principles, apart from an element of majoritarianism.

Liberal democracy contains a list of basic liberties that prevail over the will of majorities. Ronald Dworkin, for instance, only sees the decision of a majority as legitimate if it is a majority in a community of equals. He draws a distinction between 'statistical' and 'communal' democracy,[40] and suggests that communal democracy is central in all charters of rights. On this understanding a democratic decision is legitimate if people have expressed their will from a position of political equality. To this account, it is crucial to add that political equality is inconceivable without a level of basic material provision for all. This point is

---

[40] R Dworkin, *A Bill of Rights for Britain* (London, Chatto and Windus, 1990) 35.

illustrated in examples discussed earlier on in this essay. How effective is the right to vote, when someone is uneducated? Can a homeless and hungry person participate meaningfully in decision-making processes, if she constantly worries about the pressing need to survive? The concern of citizens who live in dire poverty for food and shelter gives them little space to pursue other noble goals, such as participation in democratic government. A condition of democratic governance is not only the protection of civil and political rights, but also that of social rights, without which a democracy will be imperfect. It is no accident that when there is no protection of basic needs, people feel that there is no democracy. They are justified in feeling this. Certain social and economic rights are essential conditions for political equality, which is a condition, in turn, for democracy.

Moreover, the poor and excluded might be less *willing* to participate in the political life of a society that treats them with contempt. Even more worryingly, while the destitute might be disinterested in ordinary politics and elections, the contempt that society shows to them might create in them subversive feelings towards the regime. 'People who are hungry and out of job are the stuff of which dictatorships are made', stated Franklin Roosevelt in 1936, emphasising the destructive effect that poverty may have for a democratic regime. The idea of citizenship, which was presented earlier as one of the foundations of social rights, further illustrates how civil, political and social rights are essential for membership in society. Societal isolation can inspire subversive feelings to individuals, who are not treated as members. This catastrophic effect that poverty can have is a further reminder of the links between democracy and some fundamental material necessities. Of course, the argument that social rights are a condition of democracy does not suggest that all social rights have an equally strong connection with it. It can fairly be said, though, that at least some social rights have the strongest possible links to this system of government.

Furthermore, the protection of social rights cannot be left to ordinary political processes, even in a democratic system where decisions are reached by majorities. This is because oppressive policies that neglect social rights may be exactly the result of the power that the most powerful can exert over minorities. In countries where the majority is relatively affluent, the poor and marginalised minorities have a very weak voice. The majority and their elected representatives can take decisions that neglect their interests and oppress them—decisions in which some are never given a right to express a view, or in which their view has been disregarded. On the other hand, in countries where the majority live in poverty, the poor are often ruled by a minority elite that again neglects their interests. The example of *Limbuela, Tesema and Adam*, the destitute asylum seekers of our introduction, reminds us of those who have not been represented, who have not had their voice heard and whose interests may have not been taken into account in the decisions of the majority.

The role of judicial review is partly to correct the deficiencies of democratic systems and their effect on the most vulnerable. The judiciary can protect the rights of the weak against the oppressive power of the strong and the many. Judges can question the legislative and executive power that might neglect the poorest. That they are unelected and unaccountable, unlike the government, might not in fact be a weakness. Lack of accountability to the people might be an invaluable strength. This is because the government that is concerned to be re-elected will not easily reach decisions that are unpopular in the eyes of the many or the powerful elite, due to the potential political cost of these. Judges, on the other hand, are less likely to succumb to populist pressures, unlike politicians who seek to be re-elected.

The justiciability of social rights, in other words, is compatible with democracy, and may strengthen it. Let us now consider the role of litigation in some more detail, to examine if it has potential to be inclusive and democratic.

5. *Effects of litigation*

Some sceptics suggest that litigation can be harmful to the interests of the most vulnerable. This is because only a few have actual access to a court. The majority of the poor and marginalised do not have the means to seek judicial protection. Moreover, when people do access courts, even if they win their case, the effect of the victory will be limited. The individual claim might be satisfied, but the decision will not assist others who are in a similar position.

In response to the argument that the poor and marginalised lack access to a court because litigation is expensive, it ought to be said that today the right to legal aid is recognised in many jurisdictions for those that are in economic need. The ECtHR, for instance, found that the right to legal aid is an essential component of the right to a fair trial, granted by article 6 of the ECHR.[41] In certain countries, of course, the fact that the right to legal aid exists in theory does not mean that legal aid will be granted in practice or that it will be adequate to enable everyone who is needy to pursue the judicial avenue. Pragmatic obstacles such as these should make us think how to ensure effectively in practice the commitments that we undertake in principle.

Obstacles of the type described above could also make us appreciate other ways in which a petition before a court or other body with a similar mandate already is, or has the potential to become, more inclusive. Individual petition does not necessarily mean that the interests of the individual applicant will be the only interests represented in court. Strategic litigation brought by NGOs or other activists, class actions involving collective adjudication for groups of victims, and group actions brought by associations—trade unions, for instance—on behalf of their members, can promote inclusiveness in judicial protection. Campaigners and other organisations sometimes have a right to participate in legal proceedings as amici curiae ('friends of the court'). This is possible, for example, in the ECtHR and the Inter-American Court of Human Rights. In addition, litigation can help focus a campaign on specific problems. A success in litigation, in turn, can give a fresh impetus to the campaign. A variety of different techniques in litigation create a platform for pressure,

---

[41] *Airey v Ireland* App No 6289/73 (Judgment of 9 October 1979).

which can lead to a closer engagement between the judiciary and political actors.

Regarding social rights in particular, the interesting Indian experience of public interest litigation provides us with useful insights. In this system, the Indian Supreme Court has relaxed standing requirements, allowing any member of the public to initiate proceedings on behalf of people who are poor and disadvantaged, and hence unable to access the Court. This is coupled by a flexible approach to the criteria of admissibility of complaints, which has led the Indian Court to hear cases even if applicants have not followed the formal procedure. In Europe, the European Social Charter has a Collective Complaints Protocol that gives a right to submit complaints, for non-compliance of a contracting state with the Charter, to some international organisations of employers and employees, national representative organisations of employers and employees and some international non-governmental organisations. In this way, it does not depend on an individual bringing a complaint (and there is no individual complaints procedure in any case) because the Collective Complaints Protocol empowers groups to bring claims for violations of the Charter. In examples such as the Indian and European, a court or committee can serve as a forum for debate between members of the monitoring bodies, state authorities and other organisations.

The remedies that a court can order can at the same time have an effect not only on the individual applicant, but also on others. In Europe, for instance, the ECtHR developed the idea of 'pilot judgments', which identify structural problems through individual petitions, and indicate legislative measures that can be taken to address these problems. Respondent states more generally, even without the use of pilot judgments, tend to comply with the decisions of the ECtHR by not only awarding compensation to the individual, but also by amending the legislation that led to the breach of the ECHR. In America, the Inter-American Court of Human Rights can order guarantees of non-repetition, which include an order to adopt new legislation and to implement policies and programmes that are consistent with human rights obligations.

The Constitutional Court of South Africa has also emphasised that in a country where the majority of the poor do not have the means to access courts, the courts have a special duty to create new tools and remedies. At the same time, initiating litigation has the potential to lead to mediation, which can reconcile the competing interests of the parties without being adversarial and without carrying the economic costs of the judicial process. In these different examples and in different ways, the judicial avenue can lead to a somewhat more systematic solution to the problem that is triggered by an individual case brought to a court.

The view that litigation can only bring individual justice is unduly narrow. Litigation can be more inclusive and more effective than this position suggests. Should a case be won, the individual applicant will often not be the only beneficiary. In some countries, a court order leads to an automatic amendment of the legislation or change in administrative action, which affects many. In other instances the judicial decision opens up a dialogue with the legislative and executive body. Elsewhere, even if the legislation is not automatically amended, a ruling puts political pressure on governments that might then amend the legislation which was held to be in breach of human rights law. In this way other people in a similar situation to the individual applicant benefit from the finding of a violation.

Further, a judicial decision of a court can prompt debate, attract public and media attention, inspire civil society's action and, finally, even lead to enactment of legislation. One such excellent example was a decision of the ECtHR, *Siliadin v France*,[42] which involved the appalling working conditions of a migrant domestic worker. The Court found that France breached the prohibition of slavery and servitude by not having effective legislation to criminalise such behaviour. The landmark ruling of the Court led not only to individual redress for the applicant by France; it also triggered discussions in several other national and supranational jurisdictions. Most significantly for my argument

---

[42] *Siliadin v France* App No 73316/01 (Judgment of 26 July 2005).

here, in a remarkable victory for the human rights movement, the *Siliadin* judgment was also heavily relied upon in the United Kingdom, and was one of the driving forces for the introduction of legislation criminalising slavery and forced labour in 2010.[43]

Moreover and more generally, the judicial protection of social rights in countries such as South Africa and India has led to debates on the constitutional protection of social rights in other countries, where this category of entitlements is traditionally regarded as non-justiciable. The Joint Committee on Human Rights in the United Kingdom, for example, has drawn heavily on these experiences in its report on a British Bill of Rights, which discusses the possible inclusion of some socio-economic entitlements.[44] Litigation, in other words, can have a much wider impact than individual redress.

[handwritten margin note: Cheaper and more effective at political level]

It is also important to appreciate that litigation for social rights might contribute to the quest for social justice in two further ways: first, it might raise awareness by attracting publicity that socially deprived people would not otherwise have the means and the power to attract. As a result of litigation, we become more aware, for instance, of post-apartheid socio-economic inequalities in South Africa or the plight of forced labour and sex trafficking in Europe. Second, individual claims for social justice push us all to think more deeply about the principles that should govern our society. The judicial avenue gives a claimant the opportunity to present her concern, forces state authorities to justify their action or omission, and requires courts to decide, providing moral reasons. Litigation for social rights, then, is beneficial not only for the individual or the group that brings a claim and has their voice heard. Even a wrongly decided case could be beneficial for us all, because it forces us to think harder about the decisions that our elected representatives make, and the key arguments for the principles of social justice that we adopt.

---

[43] V Mantouvalou, 'Modern Slavery: The UK Response' (2010) 39 (4) *Industrial Law Journal*.

[44] Joint Committee of Human Rights, 29th Report, Session 2007–2008, HL Paper 165-I, published on 10 August 2008, Chapter 5, para. 165 ff.

[handwritten: argues that it can create debate or effect on society; results in political process. Why not begin?]

Adjudication can make a significant contribution to the protection of social rights. It can correct some of the deficiencies of our majoritarian systems by giving voice to the poor and marginalised: an individual can have her voice heard and might receive compensation, as well as an official recognition that her treatment was unjust; the executive may be required to change its practice; sometimes the legislation will be amended following the finding of a breach, and other times a dialogue between the judiciary and other political actors begins. The judicial process more generally imposes an obligation on the authorities to justify their actions, and the judicial decision can provide reasons to the person that is suffering. Judicial reasoning can contribute to more general debates of social justice. The decision and surrounding debate can raise awareness about the particular problem that it highlights. It can also make us think harder about our principles of social justice. The justiciability of social rights in countries that have come to serve as paradigm examples in this matter, such as South Africa, can further lead to public debate in contexts where social rights are not explicitly guaranteed in the Constitution. There can be positive effects not only for the individual applicant, in other words, but also for others who are found in a similar position, as well as for the society as a whole.

C. The Role of Legislatures

Yet legalisation of social rights is much more far-reaching than protection by judicial review, and this is a point that justiciability sceptics sometimes miss. Placing all our attention on courts would provide a picture that is incomplete and impoverished. Although a judicial decision may lead to the amendment of legislation in some countries, which has an effect on a large number of people and not only on the individual applicant, the judicial protection of social rights is generally reactive. An injustice is only addressed if an individual claimant or a group brings a complaint. An exception to the reactive role of judicial review is the institution of judicial *preview*, which we find in a few countries like France or Ireland. On this model, the court examines the compatibility of legislation with the Constitution before it is implemented, and is able to assess the impact of legislation more systematically than a complaints procedure permits. However, most of the time, the decision of a court *follows* an existing injustice.

An additional matter of concern is that change triggered by successful applications might lack the systematic planning that respect for principles of social justice requires. This situation also raises questions about the distributive implications of judicial decisions on social rights, when matters that are likely to have very wide resource implications are at stake. Finally, and crucially, state inaction that leads to pervasive injustice might not be sufficiently targeted through judicial enforcement. This concern is particularly pertinent in jurisdictions such as the United States, where courts are reluctant to impose positive duties on state authorities.

In some countries, moreover, the key concern voiced in liberal scholarship is that the judiciary will simply not be open to socio-economic claims. Or that even if it is favourable to social rights claims, judges might still perceive themselves as not being able to go as far as some might believe they should, as is sometimes said about the Constitutional Court of South Africa. Faced with such situations, we would be disappointed. We would question the role of legal enforcement of social rights. We might even start questioning the point of using the term 'human rights' altogether. We would become sceptics.

However, the moral force and the transformative potential of the legalisation of social rights does not end here. It has another aspect, which is proactive rather than reactive, forward-looking rather than backward-looking. It involves the role of legislatures, and has mainly been developed by US thinkers concerned with questions of social justice. To put this debate in context, it is important to be reminded that the US Supreme Court does not recognise positive duties: according to well-established jurisprudence, duties that correspond to constitutional rights are negative, requiring minimal government action. In response to this, Robin West, for instance, has stressed that the meaning of the Constitution should not be limited to the Constitution as interpreted by courts, the adjudicated Constitution. West insightfully and forcefully analysed the role of legislatures in her discussion of the 'legislated Constitution, the Constitution looked to by the conscientious legislator as he or she seeks to fulfil her political obligations'.[45] On this analysis, it is essential to understand that principles of rights are addressed to legislators as much as to the judiciary. It is important that legislators realise that they are under a constitutional duty to treat the meeting of everyone's basic needs as an issue that has priority over other matters. It is not a party-political issue. In fact, the elected legislature has a primary duty to legislate for basic material conditions, a duty which might sometimes not be fully enforceable by the judiciary, as will be argued in the following section.

The moral, political or legal duties of legislatures have been neglected in academic scholarship on social rights, even by proponents of social rights that pay most of their attention to the potential and shortcomings of the judicial avenue. The problem, as presented by West, is that lawyers often equate moral questions to constitutional questions, constitutional questions to legal questions, and legal questions to judicial questions. On this understanding, all moral questions end up being questions that the judiciary addresses; the way that the judiciary responds to them also constitutes what the law says.[46] If the Constitution or other law of a status higher than ordinary legislation, and the relevant jurisprudence, does not impose duties to legislate for basic material conditions, these duties are non-existent both as a matter of law and as a matter of morality. In the United States, for instance, where courts entirely reject the argument that constitutional rights impose positive duties, legislators are seen as under neither a moral, political or legal obligation to act positively

---

[45] R West, 'The Missing Jurisprudence of the Legislated Constitution' in JM Balkin and RB Siegel (eds), *The Constitution in 2020* (Oxford, OUP, 2009) 79.

[46] R West, 'Unenumerated Duties' (2006) 9 *University of Pennsylvania Journal of Constitutional Law* 221, 242.

and adopt legislation that will promote welfare provision. If the adjudicated Constitution does not recognise duties to legislate for basic material conditions, these duties are not regarded as legal duties at all.

It is crucial to uncouple moral questions, such as the right to basic material conditions, from the adjudicated Constitution because constitutional principles are not solely those that the courts proclaim. There is also the Constitution that guides the political process and sets the standards towards which politics aspire, as well as those against which political decisions should be assessed. Law-making by our elected representatives ought to be full of moral ambition, and this is a point that is often missed when the judiciary is regarded as the sole virtuous branch.[47] This is an incomplete understanding not only of constitutional rights. It is, above all, an 'incomplete rendition of the social compact between state and citizen'.[48]

Instead of concentrating all our efforts on exploring, analysing and criticising courts, as many justiciability opponents and proponents often do, it is essential to turn also to the elected branch of the government. In exploring social rights, we should consider how a liberal state must act, so as to deliver its duties of social justice to its citizens, rather than neglecting the question for the sole reason that courts do not fare well in these questions. Finally, we should examine whether some constitutions or rights documents simply fail to capture the key challenges of social justice, for if they do fail, they will be clearly inadequate and this should be regarded as a moral, constitutional and political crisis.[49]

The reason that generations of lawyers have focused on courts might be explained by the fact that some have been let down by politics. The response to the sceptics of justiciability applies here with equal force: that we have sometimes witnessed populism

---

[47] R West, 'Ennobling Politics', in H Jefferson Powell and J Boyd White (eds), *Law and Democracy in the Empire of Force* (Ann Arbor, University of Michigan Press, 2009) 58.
[48] ibid 80.
[49] ibid 82.

and preferential treatment of the interests of the powerful by the legislature should not make us sceptics. We should consider instead whether the disenchantment with politics is partly due to the fact that we have constantly thought that virtue lies with courts, rather than the legislatures. Of course, the critical analysis of judicial decisions serves to identify and tackle a problem in the law. Arguments addressed to courts are in this way always indirectly addressed to the legislators too. Yet the rejection of a social rights claim by a court does not imply that there is no constitutional duty on the part of a government to deliver the relevant good to its citizens.

The position that legislators might have duties—moral, political or constitutional—to legislate for the satisfaction of basic material conditions, leads to new lines of enquiry. The key challenge is to be imaginative about how such arguments can be made in an influential manner. In some contexts, it is true that the legislative body might be more receptive to academic arguments than the courts are, though this is not necessarily so. There is a need to think how the universities, organisations which promote social justice and others can have an input to the legislative process. West suggests, for instance, that law students should be encouraged to do internships not only with judges, but also with legislators, and that university education should provide them with such possibilities. At the same time, activists in the area of social rights should turn to strategies that do not only involve courts, but also political lobbying. This already happens in India, for example, where courts are receptive to social rights claims but their decisions do not always bring about the desirable change. These are no doubt big challenges, and differ from one country to another, with their distinct legal systems, traditions and social problems, while some of the challenges that will be explored later on in this essay are global, involving duties of the affluent to the desperately needy, nearby and distant.

Social rights scholarship has focused on the role of justiciability as the main route to a more just society. In countries where courts have been unwilling to develop social rights jurisprudence, the focus on justiciability has contributed to the removal of claims of social justice from the constitutional agenda, which is problematic, for it leads to an impoverished conception of the citizen, neglecting the role of basic material conditions for well-being. In countries where courts are open to social rights claims, justiciability focuses on certain particular claims that are brought to court and not to all or even the gravest matters of social injustice. It is essential, therefore, to place attention on our elected representatives, for human rights principles embody several duties that guarantee a minimum level of subsistence in society—duties that should guide the legislative process primarily.

Mechanisms that could assist the task of the protection of social rights outside courts could include the establishment of parliamentary committees modelled on the Inter-American Commission on Human Rights, for instance, or Ombudsmen. Institutions of this type can help to identify key social rights problems. The Inter-American Commission on Human Rights has a promotional mandate, which empowers it to hold hearings on general themes, conduct on-site visits and issue recommendations and advisory opinions that have the potential to address wider questions of social justice that might not be raised by an individual petition alone. The effects of these powers of the Commission include raising awareness of potential violations of social rights in the region and complementing litigation by providing essential information. Human rights commissions at the same time can issue reports informing the government on problems of poverty and make recommendations as to how these can be addressed. Reporting procedures are common in the protection of social rights at supranational level, in the context of the ICESCR and the ESC, and have sometimes delivered significant outcomes in the development of social rights obligations. In a similar manner, Ombudsmen, who are appointed by the parliament or the government but who are independent from it, with a mandate to examine questions of socio-economic deprivation, may provide an important alternative to the adversarial model of the judicial protection of social rights, and lead to a more systematic review of the protection of social rights.

It is essential to take both the judicial and the legislative avenue for the sake of the most vulnerable amongst us. We ought to look forward and consider the duties of the legislators, who have a primary obligation to adopt legislation that promotes basic welfare provision. We also ought to look back and hold state authorities accountable for their actions and omissions that violate social rights. The action or inaction of the legislative and executive branches of government will be of judicial concern. The role of the court is to examine whether people's social rights are rightly prioritised in the legislative process and also respected by the executive branch of the government. The exact structure of the relationship between the branches of government will depend on the constitutional arrangements in each country, and particularly on the extent of judicial powers, but ideally, it should be a relationship of dialogue and partnership. Some of these issues will be analysed further in the next section.

V. CONTENT OF DUTIES AND HORIZONTALITY

The legalisation of social rights is essential in a decent society, I have argued. Social rights are claims of such urgency and importance that they should not be left to ordinary legislation and uncontrolled executive action. They ought to be protected as abstract principles in constitutions or other documents that have a distinct status. Yet, rights to the meeting of basic needs, like civil and political rights, might at first glance appear overly vague. People will naturally ask: What is a right to basic nutrition? How much water are we entitled to have? Do we have a right to a house in the countryside? Do we have a right to the job of our dreams?

Most importantly, social rights might give rise to dramatic conflicts. Clashes over the protection of resource-intensive claims are often due to scarcity of resources. Conflicts between civil, political, economic and social rights would probably be avoided if we adopted a libertarian model where rights are regarded as imposing negative duties only. If the government's sole obligation was not to interfere with a person's right to expression by not censoring her, or with someone's right to housing by not evicting her, and with someone's right to healthcare by not contaminating the land where she lives, it would be harder to envisage immediate conflicts between various rights. However, because rights to basic material provision (like civil and political rights) can also impose duties to act, a complexity emerges. The right to healthcare might require the government to provide an expensive drug for someone, which might not always be available for everyone. The provision of an expensive drug to everyone who needs it could mean that resources might be limited for free primary education of a high standard. Prioritising resources for education might reduce the resources available for the creation and monitoring of decent jobs through a system of labour inspection, for instance. Very often rights give rise to duties that impose a significant burden on the state budget, which is limited. How could limited resources and clashes between rights be addressed in interpreting social rights? Most importantly, what should the role of each branch of government be in making the correlative duties concrete?

The interests and values that underlie social rights should be able to provide some guidance. The idea of dignity, for instance, suggests that the content of social rights is minimal. Social rights do not secure a luxurious life. They form the basis for a decent life. On the issue of clashes between rights, two points ought to be made. First, because rights are grounded in urgent interests, they will always have priority over interests that do not attain the status of right. A person's right should not be balanced against the non rights-based interests of others, no matter how numerous these others are. Second, even if rights prevail over non rights-based interests, they may still clash with each other. In these instances, there will still be a need for trade-offs, which will not, however, be of the brute sort of a cost-benefit analysis.[50]

A crucial clarification is needed here. The above discussion on the legalisation of rights distinguished between the role of courts,

---

[50] See, generally, J Waldron, *Liberal Rights* (Cambridge, CUP, 1993) ch 9.

on the one hand, and the role of legislators, on the other. The sections that follow explore the legislative and judicial approaches to social rights.

A. Legislative Determination

The duties of legislative bodies in the area of social rights are wide. The content of state obligations can be illustrated by the approach of the CESCR. The CESCR, which provides authoritative interpretations of the provisions of the ICESCR, attempted to determine the content of states' obligations in General Comment No 3.[51] This aims to clarify article 2(1) of the Covenant that describes these obligations. It explains that while the fulfilment of social rights depends on the availability of resources, some of the corresponding duties, such as the prohibition of discrimination, are immediately effective. The steps that states should take towards the 'progressive realisation' of social rights, moreover, ought to be taken immediately, and be 'deliberate, concrete and targeted as clearly as possible towards meeting the obligations recognised in the Covenant'. Legislation might be essential in order to fulfil the relevant obligations; yet the state should also take all other appropriate measures. Finally, there is always a minimum core of social rights that the authorities ought to protect, which is described as follows in General Comment No 3:

> 10. [. . .] a minimum core obligation to ensure the satisfaction of, at the very least, minimum essential levels of each of the rights is incumbent upon every State party. Thus, for example, a State party in which any significant number of individuals is deprived of essential foodstuffs, of essential primary health care, of basic shelter and housing, or of the most basic forms of education is, prima facie, failing to discharge its obligations under the Covenant [. . .]

In assessing whether the state complies with its minimum core obligations, the Committee pays attention to resource constraints,

[51] CESCR General Comment No 3: 'The Nature of State Parties' Obligations' (14 December 1990).

but in order for a country to blame scarce resources for its failure to comply with the minimum core, it has to show that it has made very serious efforts to address its minimum core duties.

The example of the right to water can serve to illustrate the approach of the CESCR to the minimum core content of social rights that has an immediate effect. It shows how a right that appears to be abstract at first glance, can in fact, have a rather concrete content if thoroughly considered. The right to water is not explicitly protected in the ICESCR, but in General Comment No 15 the Committee stated that the legal basis of the right is to be found in articles 11 (right to an adequate standard of living) and 12 (right to the highest attainable standard of physical and mental health) of the Covenant. The minimum core of the right was described as follows:

(a) To ensure access to the minimum essential amount of water, that is sufficient and safe for personal and domestic uses to prevent disease; (b) To ensure the right of access to water and water facilities and services on a non-discriminatory basis, especially for disadvantaged or marginalized groups; (c) To ensure physical access to water facilities or services that provide sufficient, safe and regular water; that have a sufficient number of water outlets to avoid prohibitive waiting times; and that are at a reasonable distance from the household; (d) To ensure personal security is not threatened when having to physically access to water; (e) To ensure equitable distribution of all available water facilities and services; (f) To adopt and implement a national water strategy and plan of action addressing the whole population; the strategy and plan of action should be devised, and periodically reviewed, on the basis of a participatory and transparent process; it should include methods, such as right to water indicators and benchmarks, by which progress can be closely monitored; the process by which the strategy and plan of action are devised, as well as their content, shall give particular attention to all disadvantaged or marginalized groups; (g) To monitor the extent of the realization, or the non-realization, of the right to water; (h) To adopt relatively low-cost targeted water programmes to protect vulnerable and marginalized groups; (i) To take measures to prevent, treat and control diseases linked to water, in particular ensuring access to adequate sanitation;

The approach of the CESCR could usefully serve to determine the duties of legislators in the area of social rights.

Two questions might arise here, one involving the relationship between social rights and social justice, the other the role of economic efficiency arguments in the social rights debate. On the first matter, it is fair to say that each government will have a different conception of principles of social justice that it seeks to employ. One might follow the account of John Rawls and the 'difference principle', for instance, and consider that inequalities in the distribution of goods are permitted insofar as they work to the benefit of the worst-off.[52] What is the relationship between this principle as an account of social justice, on the one hand, and basic social rights, when addressed to courts and legislators, on the other? Social rights do not provide a full account of a theory of distributive justice; they identify some minimal requirements for a decent life that any account of social justice would have to respect and ensure. Social rights as advocated here, in other words, should form the heart of any conception of distributive justice, and would be compatible with most conceptions of social justice.

As to the relationship between social rights and economic efficiency, there is a neoclassical view of the economy according to which creating a safety net by providing for a minimum level of socio-economic provision might harm productivity. On this view, people will become idle if basic welfare is guaranteed, and this will in turn be problematic for social rights in the long-term because the reduction of productivity will result in fewer resources for all, potentially affecting the worst-off in society too. This argument is often made in the area of labour rights, for instance, where it is suggested that the creation of rigidities in the form of protective legislation of basic social rights might increase unemployment in the long-term. It ought to be stressed that this is a contested issue and there is no evidence to prove that the protection of basic rights harms productivity in reality. In fact it could be suggested that the right to education, for instance, provides the basic tools for labour

---

[52] Rawls, *Political Liberalism* (2005) 281–82.

market participation that will enhance economic flourishing. In any case, the neoliberal economic analysis, according to which basic rights undermine economic efficiency, is misleading. This is because labour regulation may in fact promote economic efficiency, while the key questions involve the degree and form of regulation.[53]

Most significantly, a government that treats people as means to an end—that of economic efficiency—is one that cannot be regarded as decent; its legitimacy is therefore questionable. Letting people suffer undernourished lives or live in unemployment and ill-health without any social support, for the reason that the market might do the work—it might promote economic flourishing and consequently create more housing, healthcare and employment in the long-run—is a position that is contrary to ideas of the basic concern and respect that a state ought to show towards its members, and goes against the grain of human rights law. Short-term human suffering for some supposed long-term goals of economic development neglects the value of the person as an individual. It is also profoundly undemocratic, if we define democracy as requiring a minimum level of social provision based on equal concern and respect. Social rights are basic preconditions for a fair society, having a central role in addressing the failures of the market, which is in any case not designed to meet the basic needs of all and might well not achieve this outcome in the long or short-run.

B. Judicial Determination

Returning to the role of courts in defining the content of social rights, it is worth mentioning again the social rights sceptics. It seems to me that many opponents of social rights do not reject the value of basic material provision. What they really dislike is the judicial protection of social rights. Yet, it is very likely that what

---

[53] S Deakin, F Wilkinson, 'Rights v Efficiency? The Economic Case for Transnational Labour Standards' (1994) 23 *Industrial Law Journal* 289.

Ireland

they have in mind when rejecting the role of courts is a particular model of judicial review: *strong judicial review*.[54] In some jurisdictions, when a court finds that legislation violates a constitutional right, it has the power to refuse to implement it in the case at hand, to declare that this legislation is unconstitutional and should therefore not apply in future disputes or even to strike it down. The United States model is a good example of strong judicial review. If we have strong review, which gives courts the power to override legislation, the judicial decision is determinative. The court has the final say on the content of state duties corresponding to rights. In cases of clashes between rights, it is fair to say that a court should refrain from being too interventionist. The elected branch of the government that is accountable to the electorate has legitimacy to reach the final decisions on resource allocation, when a case raises matters that need systematic planning and reform. Still, a court that exercises strong review should not hesitate to find a breach of social rights, when the government gives priority to interests that do not attain the status of a right over social rights.

Yet, there is an alternative model that opponents of justiciability sometimes overlook. In jurisdictions around the world, we find models of *weak judicial review*. When there is weak review, the court examines the compatibility of legislation with human rights law, but it does not have the power to strike it down or grant a remedy to the individual applicant who lodged a complaint. The judgment finding a breach of a constitutional right declares that the legislation is incompatible with human rights law. It then leaves it to the elected branch of the government to decide how it will deal with the judicial determination. Section 4 of the UK HRA provides an example of weak review. This grants certain courts the power to declare that a piece of legislation is incompatible with rights protected by the ECHR. In this context, courts cannot strike down legislation, and the government does not have a duty to amend it. The court can declare that the legislation is incompatible with human rights law, and following the finding of

[54] M Tushnet, 'Social Welfare Rights and the Forms of Judicial Review' (2003-2004) 82 *Texas Law Review* 1895, 1903.

incompatibility, a minister may use the declaration to introduce a fast-track legislative procedure to amend the legislation. Another interesting example of weak review is Canada, where courts can refuse to apply legislation that is incompatible with the rights of the Canadian Charter of Rights. However, the government is still given a power to legislate, notwithstanding the judicial decision.

Wait a second, someone might say. Isn't weak review equivalent to no review at all? Not necessarily. The experience from the United Kingdom suggests that the legislative and executive branches of government take seriously the judicial decisions that rule that legislation is incompatible with human rights law. The political pressure the Government faces following a declaration of incompatibility is significant and makes it consider how to render the legislation compatible with its human rights obligations. In Canada, the clause that allows the legislative body to legislate notwithstanding the incompatibility with rights is rarely used. These examples, therefore, suggest that in countries with weak review, the legislators do not ignore the courts' rulings.

A model of weak judicial review, in particular, may be more suitable for cases where we have clashes between rights. Here, the court can scrutinise legislation for its compatibility with human rights law, without having the final say on how resources will be distributed. This is particularly appropriate because judges might not always have the systematic knowledge or the overview of the budget that the legislative and executive branches of government have. At the same time a model of weak review can generate dialogue between the court and the legislative and executive branch of the government, as the Canadian example shows. Moreover, and more generally, it was earlier suggested that the judicial avenue does not only lead to individual justice. It also creates a forum for people to be heard, and can raise awareness about important social problems. These effects of litigation are retained even in a model of weak review.

In South Africa, in the area of socio-economic rights, the debate on strong versus weak review takes the form of a debate on a minimum core of social rights versus a 'reasonableness approach' to the decisions of the legislative and executive branch. Although the South African Constitutional Court has been urged to use the strict standard of the 'minimum core' of the CESCR, which was presented earlier, it has sometimes opted for a model of weak review. Faced with the question of the minimum core of the right to housing in the *Grootboom* case, Yacoob J stated that unlike the CESCR, which could use states' reports and other materials, it did not have the necessary information to determine it. The Court employed the standard of reasonableness instead of the minimum core. The role of the standard of reasonableness in the judicial protection of social rights, particularly when there are resource constraints, is well illustrated in the *Soobramoney v Minister of Health (KwaZulu-Natal)*[55] case. Mr Soobramoney was severely ill with chronic renal failure. He requested kidney dialysis treatment at the hospital where he was being treated, but there were not enough machines available for the necessary treatment. His request was rejected for shortage of resources. Before the Constitutional Court of South-Africa, he argued that this refusal amounted to a violation of article 27(3) of the Constitution, which provides that '[n]o one may be refused emergency medical treatment', and of the right to life. The Court ruled that the hospital's resources were reasonably allocated. The number of machines available that could treat patients with both acute and with chronic kidney failure was not adequate for all, and the decision to treat those with acute failure was justified. Chaskalson J said that 'a court should be slow to interfere with rational decisions taken in good faith by the political organs and medical authorities whose responsibility it is to deal with such matters'.[56]

The test of reasonableness aims to establish if the state measures meet several basic standards: whether they are comprehensive and coordinated, whether resources are made available, whether they are conceived and implemented in a reasonable manner, and other such issues. In *Soobramoney*, the idea was that it would be myopic to provide medical treatment only to the individual that applied

---

[55] *Soobramoney v Minister of Health (KwaZulu-Natal)* (CCT 32/97) 1997 ZACC 17.,
[56] *Soobramoney* (n 55) [29].

to the Court without taking account of the implications that the decision would have for other people's needs who were found in similar circumstances, but could not access courts. This case dramatically brings to the fore the problem of scarce resources. In a manner that illustrated the painful process of decision-making, Albie Sachs said: 'If resources were co-extensive with compassion, I have no doubt as to what my decision would have been.'[57] However, resources are limited and the judiciary decided to show deference to a decision of the authorities that it held to be reasonable. This test was recently reaffirmed in the *Mazibuko* case, which was mentioned earlier.

At the same time, although the South African Constitutional Court has sometimes opted for a weak model, it has not always shown deference to the authorities. An example where the Court found a breach of the Constitution is the *Minister of Health v Treatment Action Campaign (TAC)* case.[58] This involved the provision of the life-saving antiretroviral drug Nevirapine to women and their newborn children, which was not made generally available, only in a small number of sites in the country. The Court held that this government policy was unconstitutional, pointing to the fact that a change in the policy, which was held to be unfair, would not carry wide resource implications.

The weak model of the 'reasonableness' approach is not foreign territory for lawyers. It brings to mind debates on the proper role of unelected bodies like courts in other areas of law, such as counter-terrorism—debates which are couched in the terms of 'deference' or the 'margin of appreciation'. The notion of reasonableness alone cannot do all the work; for if courts always defer to the government, they do not really protect rights. If they always find a violation, they ignore the problem of scarcity of resources. Several scholars particularly criticise the standard used by the South African Constitutional Court for being overly deferential to the power of the legislative and executive branches of government, and others suggest that deference is the right way

---

[57] ibid [59] (Sachs J).
[58] *Minister of Health v Treatment Action Campaign* (CCT 09/02) 2002 ZACC 16.

forward for a court that needs to respect political decisions. The heart of the matter here is that a theory of what is reasonable for the government to do will be needed and the difficult question of resources will inevitably arise. The court can sometimes provide an answer, when a resource-intensive right clashes with interests that are not rights. When resource-intensive rights themselves clash, the final say should stay with the legislative and executive.

Several other principles and techniques to elucidate the content of social rights have been developed in jurisdictions around the world. A technique, which courts have sometimes employed, is what was earlier described as an 'integrated approach' to interpretation. In certain cases that involve technical labour-related matters, for instance, some courts have made use of materials of expert bodies such as the ILO and the European Committee of Social Rights, in order to determine the content of state duties. The example of the *Sidabras and Džiautas* case, which was discussed earlier, illustrates how a court can give social rights a concrete content by relying on determinations of bodies with the appropriate expertise. Of course these expert bodies will have to address similar normative issues. Yet they might be better equipped in dealing with them because of their longer experience. The adoption of the integrated approach is valuable in that it helps make the content of social rights more concrete by providing insights in areas where courts might not always have the necessary expertise.

Which is the most appropriate test, a strong or a weaker one? To determine the content of social rights when decided by the judiciary depends on the interests that are in conflict. Considerations involving scarce resources when rights clash might legitimately compel a court to let the government decide, insofar as this decision can be supported by fair principles. A clearly unprincipled policy, which restricts a social right, say the right to education, to children of a particular race for instance, would be unjustified in all circumstances, and should always be found to be unconstitutional. In addition, as it was said earlier, while the court might not be able to prescribe how resources should be allocated when rights clash, it should be able to determine that a certain level of socio-economic provision resists trade-offs when there is a conflict with policy considerations that do not attain the status of rights.

Suffice it to say that social rights can obtain a clear content, as much as civil and political rights can; that legislatures have wider obligations than courts; and that courts should hold them accountable if they fail to deliver their primary duties to basic social provision, without necessarily being overly intrusive. In addition, it is important to keep in mind that the definition of social rights as rights to the satisfaction of basic needs does not require an endorsement of the minimum core approach by the judiciary, exactly because when rights clash, what the courts can order might be more limited than what the legislature can decide.

The heart of the argument in this section can be stated as follows: courts and other bodies with judicial functions should not show excessive activism in individual cases when faced with clashes between rights, in cases that might have a systematic impact on the allocation of resources to other poor and needy individuals that cannot access courts. However for legislators, social rights should be regarded as an absolute priority. The exact degree of this duty would be subject to disagreement, of course, but a minimum level of socio-economic provision provided by the state as a safety net can obtain a certain degree of objectivity and concreteness, and can be determined either by the government alone and working with non-judicial bodies, or by courts in partnership with the government. It can be fairly said, however, that in a manner similar to civil and political rights, social rights can be rendered concrete through systematic engagement, moral and legal argument on the scope of their correlative duties; and that the elaboration of this content can be both subject to judicial and to legislative work.

C. Horizontal Application

Traditionally, the legal protection of human rights involved the relationship between the individual and the state. Civil and political rights, such as the prohibition of torture or the right to free expression, and social and economic rights, like the right to housing or the right to healthcare, were initially developed to protect individuals against government. The right of individuals to turn against their own state authorities was considered to be revolutionary in international law. To a large extent, this body of law had to do with interstate relations, often involving treaties containing state rights and obligations. The individual did not appear in the picture. Human rights law brought the individual into the system, who was for the first time empowered to turn against state authorities. At national level too, constitutional rights were rights of the individual primarily against the state, in a manner similar to international human rights law.

Today, the legalisation of social rights does not only affect the relationship between the individual and the state. The vertical model that sees human rights as restricting state power against the individual appears to be wanting, and human rights law has developed in ways that attempt to address the inadequacies. In the world of the market economy, it becomes increasingly evident that significant threats to people's access to basic necessities stem from private actors. The problem is often not state action, but state abstention. When the state remains inactive, market pressures and private economic interests take priority and act unregulated. Multinational enterprises that have income higher than the gross national product of certain developing countries, invest in poor areas and pursue economic gain while ignoring or harming the interests of local communities and individuals. Examples of where these kinds of activities affect social and labour rights are ample. As human rights law stood at its inception, little could be done to hold private actors directly accountable for violations of rights because most international human rights treaties and national constitutions regulated state rather than private conduct.

In response to the problem of non-state actors' power, in several national contexts it is increasingly accepted that human rights law applies horizontally too, between private parties, and not only between the state and the individual. In Germany, for instance, the Constitutional Court developed the doctrine of *Drittwirkung*, according to which constitutional rights may bind private parties. These rights cannot be invoked by individuals against each other directly, but they can be invoked as interpretive principles in the application of legislation that regulates relations between private parties. In this way the German Constitutional Court interprets private law in a manner that reflects the values that underlie constitutional rights. In the United Kingdom, the HRA imposes an obligation on courts and public authorities to act in accordance with the rights of the Convention, and a further duty on courts to interpret national legislation in a manner that makes it compatible with the HRA. In a manner that bears similarities to the German model, the HRA has an 'indirect horizontal effect'. It does not allow private individuals to sue other private individuals directly for breach of the HRA. It permits them to rely on other existing legislation which courts will interpret in light of the rights of the HRA. If someone is dismissed for her private activities, for instance, she can rely on the legislation that prohibits unfair dismissal and argue that dismissal is unfair because it violates her right to private life under the HRA. In this way, even though the HRA does not contain social rights as such, through its horizontal application, it has an effect on legislation that embodies socio-economic principles. In this context, courts increasingly take note of human rights law in interpreting legislation so as to give effect to Convention rights. The South-African Constitution which protects socio-economic rights provides for wide horizontal effect, stating in article 8(2) that 'a provision of the Bill of Rights binds a natural or a juristic person if, and to the extent that, it is applicable, taking into account the nature of the right and the nature of any duty imposed by the right'.

The extension of human rights principles in the regulation of private relationships is a positive development that reflects the idea that human rights law incorporates certain fundamental values of a legal order, which should be equally respected in private and public law relationships. Constitutional law scholars have welcomed the extension of constitutional rights to the private sphere.[59] The development of principles of human rights in a manner that affects the relationship between private parties has also been particularly welcomed by scholars, who are concerned with principles of social justice in private law. Hugh Collins, for instance, suggested that there is a need to reconsider the values that guide private law in light of human rights principles. He urges, in particular, that social rights be afforded sufficient attention in judicial reasoning, when judicial decisions on private relationships have distributive implications.[60] The trend of interpreting private law in light of human rights principles is sometimes called the 'constitutionalisation of private law'.

A similar indirect effect of human rights principles between private parties has been developed in international law. As stated earlier, international human rights law initially involved the obligations of the state towards private parties. It had a vertical effect, and imposed negative duties of non-interference on state authorities. Yet it slowly emerged both in theory and in the jurisprudence of courts that the protection of civil and political rights also imposes positive obligations on state actors. The ECtHR, for instance, has developed a doctrine of positive obligations which is now well-established in its case law. According to this, the Convention sometimes requires state authorities to take positive action in order to regulate relationships between private parties or otherwise the state will be in breach of its treaty obligations. The *Siliadin* case, which was mentioned earlier, exemplifies this. This involved a Togolese national, who was employed as a domestic worker in France. Her employers, private individuals, held her in conditions of 'modern slavery'. They withheld Ms Siliadin's passport, and kept her isolated and unpaid, in inhuman working conditions. Before the ECtHR, Ms Siliadin argued that France was in breach of article 4 of the ECHR that prohibits slavery, servitude, forced and compulsory labour, because it did

[59] See, for instance, M Kumm, 'Who is Afraid of the Total Constitution? Constitutional Rights as Principles and the Constitutionalization of Private Law' (2006) 7 *German Law Journal* 341.

[60] H Collins, 'Utility and Rights in Common Law Reasoning: Rebalancing Private Law through Constitutionalization' (2007) 30 *Dalhousie Law Journal* 1.

not have in place effective legislation to criminalise the employers' behaviour. The Court held that France violated the Convention. Having no legislation in place to criminalise the unacceptable private conduct was in breach of human rights law.

The regulation of relationships between private parties, in the way that it has evolved at international and national level, still relies much on the role of the state. Both at domestic and at supranational level, there is often an indirect, rather than a direct horizontal effect. Although this is not necessarily problematic, it might be best also to consider how private actors can be held directly accountable for their acts that harm human rights interests.

Another distinction that is important for our discussion is that between hard law, namely legally binding documents such as treaties, and soft law, which consists of materials that have no legally binding effect, such as declarations. In international law there is a willingness to adapt to changing circumstances by creating obligations for private actors through soft law initiatives. One illustration of such an attempt to impose certain duties directly on private actors is to be found in the UN Global Compact.[61] The Global Compact, which was initiated in 2000, encourages companies to participate in and commit themselves to certain principles that will guide their operation. These principles contain a commitment to human rights and labour standards, including freedom of association and the prohibition of child labour. To this we should add further initiatives of international organisations, such as the ILO Tripartite Declaration of Principles concerning Multinational Enterprises and the Organisation for Economic Cooperation and Development (OECD) Guidelines for Multinational Enterprises, which contain certain core labour rights. In addition, there are certain private initiatives in the form of corporate codes of conduct, whereby enterprises undertake to comply with key labour rights in their relationships with their employees, their suppliers and customers.

These developments in corporate social responsibility bring human rights obligations into private companies' vocabulary

---

[61] For details on this initiative, see www.unglobalcompact.org/.

that would have probably been dominated by financial profit. Of course, the most significant weakness of soft law and other private initiatives is that their effectiveness is questionable, as much relies on the corporation itself. It might decide to adhere to the relevant principles and adopt its own principles, but it might also choose to ignore them altogether. No monitoring body would hold it accountable for violations and impose sanctions. At the same time, private initiatives lack the systematisation that monitoring of business conduct for human rights compliance requires. The shortcomings were highlighted in the Report of the Special Representative of the Secretary General on the Issue of Human Rights and Transnational Corporations and Other Business Enterprises,[62] John Ruggie, who stressed the need for more effective access to remedies.

Yet, it can fairly be argued that corporate codes of conduct constitute a positive first step in response to the changing needs of globalised market economies. The legal protection of social rights should be open to such soft law initiatives. This is because these developments, taken together with other hard law initiatives, exhibit how different modes of regulation that intersect might contribute to reaching the desired outcomes.[63] The corporate codes of conduct apply to activities of private actors, including multinational enterprises, which the international or national human rights framework would most probably not be able to capture. In this way they contribute to the promotion of human rights principles in the private sphere and in the extra-territorial activities of companies, that have to comply with them or they would otherwise attract negative publicity that would harm their economic interests.

In legalising social rights to regulate private conduct, the distinction between hard and soft law takes on an important role, to conclude. In the area of legally binding obligations, social rights

[62] Report entitled 'Protect, Respect and Remedy: a Framework for Business and Human Rights' (7 April 2008) A/HRC/8/5.
[63] P Macklem, 'Labour Law beyond Borders' (2002) 5 *Journal of International Economic Law* 605.

have sometimes acquired a horizontal effect, reshaping private law in light of constitutional principles. Here both domestic law in many jurisdictions and international human rights law tend to hold private actors accountable indirectly by imposing positive obligations on state authorities to regulate private activity. When it comes to soft law, initiatives that encourage private actors to comply with certain fundamental standards are positive, not for their effectiveness (which might be limited), but mainly for their complementary role in the regulation of private conduct that hard law does not reach. A combination of public and private, hard law and soft law initiatives should be showing the way ahead in dealing with unequal relationships between private parties.

VI. SOCIAL RIGHTS AND THE FOREIGN NEEDY

In what has been considered so far, the main focus was on duties of the state imposed by social rights in national and international law towards people that live within its borders. We examined the role of courts and the role of legislatures in the legalisation of social rights, in order to assess how the relevant duties can best be delivered by the different powers. Yet by uncoupling legalisation from justiciability, we are better able to explore the big challenges with which the law on social rights has the potential to assist— challenges that ought to be addressed by our legislators primarily. These involve the social rights of the desperately needy foreigner.

Although in this essay we did not distinguish between nationals and non-nationals, the law frequently does. In our globalised world, though, my clothes may have been made in India; yours in Singapore. My laptop may have been assembled in China; your coffee maker in Bangladesh. My neighbours in London may come from Canada, my friends from Brazil, and my colleagues from South Africa. At a time when national borders have become less relevant than in the past, and that economic interaction and mobility between states is much more intense than ever before, concentrating the discussion of legalisation on the duties that we owe to our fellow nationals or those that lawfully reside within our borders is myopic. If social rights are based on universal values, shouldn't everyone be entitled to a basic level of socio-economic provision? If everyone is so entitled, how does our legal system fare in assigning the correlative duties?

This final section turns on the global challenge that the legalisation of social rights faces. It identifies gaps in the law and suggests that addressing duties towards non-nationals in the current legal framework is an area of priority, first for legislators when legislating, but also for courts when adjudicating. The key idea in this part is that we should no longer distinguish between nationals and foreign citizens. We should instead endorse a different dichotomy in the elaboration of the question to whom duties are owed: a distinction between the 'nearby' and the 'distant needy'. The primary obligation to reconsider the scope of the law in this respect falls on the legislators who need to reform the domestic legal framework and reconsider the international institutional arrangements, although, as we will see, courts have sometimes successfully tackled these difficult questions. The law on duties to the nearby and the distant needy foreigner will be the subject of the two sections that follow.

A. Duties to the Nearby Needy

The law on social rights should no longer distinguish between nationals and foreigners that live in a state. Why do we have special obligations to those that are within our borders, both fellow nationals and foreigners? In 'Moral Closeness and the World Community', Richard Miller stated that '[o]rdinary moral thinking about aid to needy strangers discriminates in favor of the political closeness of compatriots and the literal closeness of people in peril who are close at hand'.[64] The idea of closeness is based either on the fact that we have special relationships with various people, such as members

---

[64] R Miller, 'Moral Closeness and the World Community' in DK Chatterjee (ed), *The Ethics of Assistance: Morality and the Distant Needy* (Cambridge, CUP, 2004) 101.

of our family and friends or compatriots and others that belong to our community, which justify the intuition that we owe special duties to them; or on geographical proximity with someone who is in danger which, coupled with knowledge of this danger, might give rise to special obligations. Obligations stemming from these two types of proximity make the different treatment of our close ones morally defensible; the special relations that we have with those that are close to us explain the position that we have a stronger duty to aid them when they are in need, without foreclosing duties to assist the distant needy too. This is also supported by the current institutional arrangements. The world order is comprised of states and is organised around the institutions of these states. The idea of citizenship, moreover, which was mentioned earlier as a basis of civil, political and social rights, reflects the view that the ties between members of a particular society may be stronger than the ties that we have with those living in remote locations.

In human rights law too, it is sometimes recognised that a country might owe certain duties to someone because that person is within its borders, because she is nearby and in peril—obligations that would not be owed if she were in a remote location. The 'non-refoulement' cases illustrate how both of the above types of proximity can be combined: according to a well-established principle in human rights and refugee law, state authorities must not return someone to her country if that person is likely to be subjected to torture or inhuman and degrading treatment on return.[65] States have human rights obligations towards her only because she is within their borders. If that same person faced a similar threat while in her home-country, responsibility would not arise for the actions of a foreign government. Physical proximity combined with a risk of harm if the person is deported could be described as giving rise to 'a duty to rescue' the individual that would be imperilled if extradited or expelled.

Unsurprisingly, the law on social rights often fails to capture the important principle of duties that we owe to the nearby needy,

---

[65] See, for instance, *Soering v UK* App No 14038/88 (Judgment of 7 July 1989).

which we find in the jurisprudence of civil and political rights. Even in countries that protect the rights of the economically weak and vulnerable in their constitutions or that have signed up to treaties that monitor the implementation of social rights, there is a striking problem: there is a sharp divide between the insider and the outsider. To the question of who is entitled to social provision, the answer is usually: the country's own nationals only. Civil rights are afforded to everyone within a state's jurisdiction, political rights to some non-nationals too. Social rights suffer. They are frequently guaranteed only to the nationals of a state or sometimes its permanent residents, while undocumented migrants remain excluded.

The reasons that are supposed to justify the discrepancy in the personal scope of social rights rest on the institutional structure of the state. We, nationals of the country where we live, vote for our government, contribute to the economy, and are taxed. Hence, we are entitled to welfare provision that those that have not borne similar burdens are not entitled to receive. Human rights law sometimes reflects the view that foreign nationals are rightly excluded from rights to the satisfaction of their basic needs by that state. This is illustrated in the Appendix to the ESC which, under the title 'Scope of the Social Charter in Terms of Persons Protected', states:

> . . . persons covered by Article 1 to 17 include foreigners only insofar as they are nationals of other Contracting Parties lawfully resident or working regularly within the territory of the Contracting Party concerned, subject to the understanding that these Articles are to be interpreted in the light of the provisions of Articles 18 and 19.

Most provisions of the ESC do not cover other residents and lawfully employed persons. Article 19, entitled 'The Right of Migrant Workers and their Families to Protection and Assistance', incorporates labour rights for migrant workers. The main characteristic of this provision is that while it requires certain measures to protect migrants that live and work in the contracting parties, it does not guarantee protection equal to that accorded to the state's own nationals. Moreover, article

19, like the rest of the Charter's articles, is not binding upon all Member States of the Charter, but only upon those that decide to sign up to it. This means that a state can decide to neglect even foreign nationals working lawfully in a country altogether. More strikingly, work-related rights depend upon the status of immigrants as lawful residents, which means that persons residing and working illegally in the territory of contracting states will not enjoy any protection of their social rights whatsoever.

The problems posed by the narrow personal scope of the ESC became particularly evident in a decision of the European Committee of Social Rights, *International Federation of Human Rights Leagues (FIDH) v France*.[66] Here the lack of access to healthcare for children of undocumented migrants was held to be in breach of the protection of children and young persons, contrary to the clear wording of the Charter that excludes non-nationals. This was because, on the reasoning of the Committee, to hold otherwise would be contrary to human dignity, which constitutes one of the Charter's most fundamental underlying values. The exclusion of foreign-national permanent residents and their children from access to social assistance was successfully challenged in South Africa too, where the Court paid special attention to the fact that this group of individuals contributed to the national economy and were taxed. Their legislative exclusion was held to breach both the prohibition of discrimination and the right of everyone to have access to social assistance.[67] These developments reflect the deep problem that is created by the exclusion of vulnerable individuals from basic socio-economic provision. The fact that monitoring bodies are compelled in certain circumstances to reach decisions that conflict with the clear wording of the documents, like the case of the ESC in particular, simply emphasises the compelling need to revise their unjustifiably narrow personal scope, which should form a priority in the legalisation of social rights.

[66] *International Federation of Human Rights Leagues (FIDH) v France*, Complaint No 14/2003, Decision of 8 September 2004.

[67] *Khosa v Minister for Social Development* (CCT 12/03) 2004 ZACC 11.

In a different context, the US Supreme Court took a step in the opposite direction to the bodies mentioned above. In its ruling *Hoffman Plastic Compounds v NLRB*,[68] the Court held by a five to four majority that undocumented migrant workers, unlawfully dismissed because of union membership, were not entitled to compensation for their dismissal. In response, the Inter-American Court of Human Rights issued an advisory opinion on the 'Legal Condition and Rights of Undocumented Migrant Workers'.[69] In its landmark opinion, the Court held that making the right to be awarded compensation for dismissal conditional upon the status of someone as lawfully resident in the country, excluding undocumented migrants, breaches the American Convention on Human Rights. It stated:

> If undocumented workers are contracted to work, they immediately are entitled to the same rights as all workers. This is of maximum importance, since one of the major problems that come from lack of immigration status is that workers without work permits are hired in unfavorable conditions, compared to other workers.

Excluding from social rights protection those who are unlawfully employed in a country is problematic. Although some might not be taxed like the country's nationals and lawful residents who are employed therein, undocumented migrants contribute to the economy through their labour and are often occupied in jobs that nationals or lawful residents would not be willing to do. Because of their illegal status, they are extremely vulnerable to exploitation, as the earlier example of *Siliadin* reminded us. An effective system of basic social provision as a safety net is the least that ought to be done. Of course, implementation will be a great challenge here, as the key problem with undocumented migrants is that they often are, and wish to remain 'invisible' to the authorities for fear of arrest and expulsion. Yet the acknowledgment that they should be granted some social rights is a crucial step to be

[68] *Hoffman Plastic Compounds v NLRB* 535 US 137 (2002).

[69] Inter-American Court of Human Rights, 'Legal Condition and Rights of Undocumented Migrant Workers' (17 September 2003) Advisory Opinion OC-18/03.

taken. The second step will be to consider how these can best be realised.

The problem of the exclusion of foreign nationals was illustrated in the case of *Limbuela, Tesema and Adam* that was presented in the introduction of this essay. This issue becomes particularly acute in certain dramatic situations where asylum seekers require basic but systematic welfare provision. The Grand Chamber of the ECtHR has had to deal with one such situation in the important case *N v UK*.[70] This involved the return to her country of origin of a Ugandan national who needed medical treatment because she was HIV-positive. Ms N lived in the United Kingdom for many years while her asylum application was pending and received the necessary treatment for her condition. She claimed that, should she be returned to Uganda, she would suffer and die within a year or two because she would not receive this treatment there. If she were allowed to stay in the United Kingdom, on the other hand, she would live a decent life for years to come. Before the ECtHR, she argued that her deportation, which would result in the dramatic deterioration of her health, her severe suffering and death, would constitute inhuman and degrading treatment contrary to the ECHR. The majority of the Court rejected her claim, in a judgment that has been criticised for its reasoning that did not pay sufficient attention to the duties of the affluent towards foreign nationals when they are threatened with extreme suffering if returned to their country of origin. The key problem with the position taken by the majority of the Court, which ruled that deportation was lawful, is that it failed to appreciate that states sometimes have different, stronger, duties towards foreigners that are close by. For this reason we might have a 'duty to rescue' them if they, like Ms N, are in severe danger, rather than either sitting idly by or taking positive action to deport her.[71] The judges who dissented from the majority decision pointed at the shortcomings of the reasoning of the majority and suggested that

[70] *N v UK* App No 26565/05 (Grand Chamber Judgment of 27 May 2008).
[71] See V Mantouvalou, '*N v UK*: No Duty to Rescue the Nearby Needy?' (2009) 71 *Modern Law Review* 815.

the key reason that led the Court to reject the claim of Ms N was a 'floodgates argument'. The majority of the Court was concerned that upholding this complaint would lead to an influx of medical asylum seekers, which would set a heavy burden on resources. On the view of the dissenting judges, this concern was not justified. Yet the majority of the Court avoided exploring the question of numbers, and opted instead to draw a sharp line between civil and social rights.

It is important to emphasise that the idea of citizenship, which was earlier presented as one of the foundations of social rights, does not conflict with the argument that foreign nationals have social rights. Immigrants are new citizens; they are not non-citizens. This is because citizenship in the sense used here is not a synonym for nationality. It is a normative concept that emphasises the importance of rights for membership and belonging of everyone in a society, which ideas such as liberty and dignity might not be able to capture. It also explains how someone who is not a member of a society, because she is in a country only temporarily, may be entitled to a lower degree of social provision that those that live permanently therein.

The outright exclusion from the protection of social rights of foreign nationals that lawfully reside and might also work in a country is unjustified. It fails to appreciate the importance of rights to the satisfaction of basic needs for societal membership and neglects the role of foreign nationals for the flourishing of a community. The law on social rights should recognise that undocumented migrants who are employed should not be excluded from welfare provision. Even though they are unlawfully in the country, they probably still contribute significantly with their labour and are taxed. Even those that do not work in the marketplace (domestic carers, for instance) contribute to societal well-being with their labour, performing tasks that the nationals of the state would be unwilling to perform. As to the foreigner who has only stayed in a country for a very short time and is not employed, it could fairly be said that she still has certain social rights and that we still owe duties to her: perhaps not to provide social security, but duties arising if, for example, this person is at risk of death or other severe harm should she not receive the necessary social support. The basis for social rights is not only societal membership; dignity is another foundation of social rights. The indiscriminate exclusion of the nearby needy from basic welfare provision, which we sometimes find in the legal framework, is an urgent matter to tackle. Our legislators have a duty to deal with it as a matter of priority.

B. Duties to the Distant Needy

The discussion of social rights in law would be incomplete if limited to the interpretation of human rights documents, and not extended to other parts of international law that affect people's basic needs. Perhaps the most striking problems in the international human rights framework emerge when we think about the distant needy in the current world order, where large numbers of people are living in conditions of extreme poverty. This is another area that social rights sceptics neglect, by excessively focusing on justiciability. Such is the scale of the shortcomings here that the drive for change cannot come from courts. Our laws and our institutions have a long way to go before they satisfy social rights standards in the global order. The great challenges that the world order faces in order to become more just and respectful of the social rights of the global poor can only be tackled by our legislators.

The harsh reality is that most of the world's wealth is controlled by a small number of developed countries, while the developing world is suffering in socio-economic need. According to some 2008 estimates of the World Bank, 1.4 billion people in developing countries live on less than US$1.5 a day;[72] 24,000 children die daily

---

[72] S Chen and M Ravallion, 'The Developing World is Poorer that we Thought, but no Less Successful in the Fight Against Poverty' available at http://papers.ssrn.com/sol3/papers.cfm?abstract_id=1259575.

from preventable, poverty-related, causes;[73] about one billion people entered the twenty-first century illiterate. According to the United Nations, about 854 million people worldwide go to bed hungry every night. The numbers are daunting. Does the law on social rights impose any legal obligations on citizens of affluent countries to satisfy the rights of the distant needy? If not, should it do so?

In the current international human rights framework there is very little on the question of duties to the distant needy. Article 23 of the ICESCR provides as follows:

> The States Parties to the present Covenant agree that international action for the achievement of the rights recognized in the present Covenant includes such methods as the conclusion of conventions, the adoption of recommendations, the furnishing of technical assistance and the holding of regional meetings and technical meetings for the purpose of consultation and study organized in conjunction with the Governments concerned.

There is no enforceable provision about relationships between states couched in terms of rights. Questions about the rights of poor countries and the duties of more affluent ones are also discussed in the context of the 'right to development', which has been on the United Nation's agenda over the last few years. The global social rights and development agendas share common purposes, as is evident in the UN Millennium Development Goals,[74] which include the eradication of extreme poverty.

Is the lack of legal duties imposed by the key human rights documents on states to assist the global poor morally justified? In addressing the question whether there may be any moral duties to assist the distant needy, scholars commonly seek to establish some sort of causation between the economic well-being in affluent countries and the plight of poverty in the developing world. On one view, affluent societies owe no obligations to those that live in remote locations, for they did nothing to harm them or because

---

[73] See www.unicefusa.org/.
[74] UN Millennium Development Goals, available at www.un.org/millenniumgoals/.

the developing world consented to whatever behaviour resulted in the harm they now suffer.

It can fairly be said that whether affluent countries have acted or omitted to act in ways that caused harm to the distant needy is far from straightforward. Examples of historical injustice are plenty, though there may be difficulties in establishing causation between these and contemporary inequalities. Colonisation is only one such instance. Further examples of current economic exploitation of the distant needy by the affluent are also abundant. Powerful economic actors engage in economic activity in poor countries with authoritarian regimes, exploiting the natural resources and dramatically deteriorating the life of local communities. Economists note that many countries very rich in natural resources have very poor populations; natural resources do not form the basis for development, but for impoverishment. This is the so-called 'resource curse'. Rich enterprises, moreover, prefer countries with very low labour standards in order to increase their economic gain by using cheap labour. It is true that work in poor conditions in these countries might seem better than no work at all. However, the level of exploitation that is sometimes witnessed in some factories, which are known as 'sweatshops', in pursuit of economic gain—extremely low wages, overtime, unsafe working conditions—is incompatible with the core human rights values. There are, in other words, plenty of instances that might serve to show nowadays that the developed world bears responsibility for poverty in the developing world, either through action or through omission to act.

In any case, social rights towards the distant needy might better be seen as imposing duties even if there is no previous harmful act on the part of the affluent world. They are universal goals of high priority for the international community just as they are constitutional essentials at domestic level. Duties towards the distant needy exist because of the urgency of the needs of the global poor, on the one hand, coupled with the ability to pay of the affluent, on the other.[75]

---

[75] C Beitz and RE Goodin, 'Basic Rights and Beyond' in C Beitz and RE Goodin (eds), *Global Basic Rights* (Oxford, OUP, 2009) 1 at 16.

If rights to the satisfaction of basic needs are universal in a normative sense, which requires that they be enjoyed by everyone, are the duties universal too? How could these be delivered? It could be said that each one of us has a moral duty to alleviate poverty by giving out some of her property to the world's poor. Yet to suggest that each person has a duty to give some money to each hungry child might be too burdensome. It is impossible for an individual alone to bring about the necessary change that is essential for the satisfaction of the needs of the global poor. In addition, if duties to the global poor were left on individual charity, the division of labour might not be fair, as some people might end up bearing heavier costs than others.

It is crucial, instead, that our legislators focus on institutions when legalising social rights at supranational level. Courts are very unlikely to be an appropriate forum for such questions, particularly through individual petition systems. But of course the role of law is not exhausted by judicial enforcement. Here we need other institutions that will play the role of 'mediators', as Henry Shue suggested.[76] The proper role of social rights is to serve as normative standards that render concrete the duties of the duty-bearers towards the rights-holders. Existing institutions would have to assume these duties or new institutions would have to be set up with this aim.

The current international institutional architecture falls short of the ideal institutional structure. In fact, it can be said that it plays a great role in harming the most vulnerable. This is illustrated by international economic law. The World Trade Organisation (WTO), for instance, promotes free trade between its members. It establishes rules for global trade and has effective monitoring machinery. A suggestion that has been advanced, but never given effect within the WTO framework, is to include a 'social clause' in world trade agreements, which would link trade and labour rights, operating as a condition for economic transactions. Opponents of the social clause suggest that the ILO, rather than the WTO,

---

[76] H Shue, 'Mediating Duties' (1988) 98 *Ethics* 687.

should be promoting labour rights as it is a specialist organisation. One of the problems with this position is that the ILO has no real teeth to enforce labour rights. On the other hand, if a requirement to comply with social rights were tied to international trade agreements, states would be more willing to abide because of the economic implications in case they failed to take labour rights into account. Today, there are certain trade agreements that include labour rights, such as the North America Free Trade Agreement between Canada, the United States and Mexico. Although these have been criticised for being ineffective, they at least take the question of labour rights beyond purely domestic regulation and illustrate how they are and should be of international concern.

Another international economic institution, the World Bank, was created in the aftermath of the Second World War. Its aim was to help with the economic re-making of Europe and to provide funds to promote development of poor countries. The Bank could be described as the closest the international community has so far got to acting upon a duty to assist the distant needy. Is it accountable for its actions, though, when they have a negative effect on people in developing countries? To address concerns about the impact of the projects that it funds on local communities, it created the World Bank Inspection Panel, the first effort of an international financial institution to have an accountability framework for its actions. This mechanism provides a forum for people affected by a project funded by the Bank to lodge a complaint. The mandate of the Inspection Panel is to investigate whether the aid given to support a project complies with the Bank's policies and procedures and to issue recommendations. The Panel is an advisory body; it cannot provide a remedy nor can it stop a project. The report that the Panel produces is addressed to the Board of Executive Directors and Bank Management, which consider and publicise it. Even though this accountability mechanism was revolutionary for a financial institution, it has shortcomings, including the fact that it cannot investigate actors other than the Bank itself. Nevertheless, even though the Panel cannot examine the compatibility of the Bank's projects with social rights, it still raises awareness on questions of compliance with social rights. In recent years, moreover, the World Bank has been developing a more elaborate human rights agenda, linking rights and development.

The international intellectual property regime, on the other hand, might provide further evidence of lack of accountability for protection of the social rights of the global poor in current institutional arrangements. The 1994 Agreement on Trade-Related Aspects of Intellectual Property Rights (TRIPS) imposes on states an obligation to offer 20-year patents for various innovations, including pharmaceuticals. The problem with intellectual property rights is that they make the drugs and vaccines they protect very expensive. As a result, populations in developing countries that urgently need them cannot afford them. The United Nations has been very critical of TRIPS, particularly with regard to its impact on economic and social rights. The Sub-Commission on the Promotion and the Protection of Human Rights, for instance, adopted Resolution 2000/7 on 'Intellectual Property Rights and Human Rights', which recommended that human rights should be given primary attention when developing this kind of agreement. This non-binding Resolution was followed by numerous initiatives that further developed and specified how intellectual property arrangements can comply with human rights law. In 2005, the CESCR adopted General Comment No 17 on the matter, which makes certain recommendations to Member States of the ICESCR, including a recommendation that they attempt to prevent very high costs for essential medicines.

No doubt our legislators and the international community ought to do a great deal in order to make such institutional arrangements more just. In response to the problem of the impact of intellectual property rights under TRIPS on social rights, for example, it has been suggested that a 'Health Impact Fund' be created.[77] The idea is that this Fund would be financed by states and would offer pharmaceutical companies the option of registering products. Companies that did so would have to make the product available

[77] For detailed analysis, see T Pogge, 'The Health Impact Fund and its Justification by Appeal to Human Rights' (2009) 40 *Journal of Social Philosophy* 542.

wherever it was needed at the lowest possible cost for 10 years, and would then have to allow free generic production and distribution. In return for this, the innovator would get annual reward payments that would be made according to the global health impact of the product. The Health Impact Fund would also support the creation of new medicines that would be expected to have a high impact. In this way, the initiative would benefit both the poorer parts of the world that are trapped in a cycle of poverty and ill-health, and those that are well-off, by rewarding the innovators according to the impact of their products. The payments to the innovators would address the economic argument that lower costs for medicines would limit the ability of pharmaceutical firms to invest in research and develop medicines that might save many lives. Suggestions, such as the Health Impact Fund, have the significant advantage of feasibility, particularly if the alternative is to revise the state-centred international legal order radically and to create a global state with an independent accountability mechanism. The Health Impact Fund does not depend on a radically new global institutional architecture. Yet the efficacy of such proposals in delivering essential goods would need to be carefully tested.

The problems in the institutional design of the global order are not only limited to international economic law. Another matter that should crucially be considered in the legalisation of social rights in the world order is immigration. Is there a plausible alternative to the current framework that regulates international economic migration—a framework that would pay more attention to the social rights of those that live in extreme poverty? This may be one of the more promising issues for global redistribution because it offers more chance of change than other areas. It is also the one that most tests the idea of the duty to the distant needy because the accommodation that a rich society would have to make is greater, if it is willing to accept economic migrants. On this matter, scholars have convincingly argued that the gain for developed countries by a revised, much less restrictive immigration policy is far greater than the costs that neoliberal economists argue this would impose. Trebilcock, for instance, suggests that the concern that migrant labour leads to increased unemployment and lower wages in the host country is misleading, and that more liberal immigration policies than the ones currently espoused by the developed world would be beneficial both for outsiders (the immigrants) and the insiders (people in the host state).[78] He suggests that a less restrictive global immigration regime should be coupled with a private market insurance system for immigrants to protect host states against demands by immigrants for non-contributory social benefits. Other suggestions to create alternatives to the current immigration system include the proposal to set up a World Migration Organisation, a supranational body that would promote 'best practices' in immigration and encourage states to adopt more open immigration policies.[79] The heart of this matter is that rich countries need to explore the effects of restrictive immigration policy in more depth, showing consideration for the global poor and making efforts to accommodate them in their own countries—a change that, if properly thought through, would be beneficial for both the needy and the affluent in the long-run.

The revision of immigration policies and many other vastly complex questions demonstrate the difficulties with which our legislators and the international community are faced in addressing the question of global social rights and the duties of the affluent towards the distant needy. What is clear is that international institutions and the framework of accountability for violations of social rights are extremely underdeveloped compared to those at the national level. The social rights debate often appears to be of a very marginal importance. This appears to be so not only because there is no global state, but also because there is a common view that affluent countries do not owe duties to the distant needy—a position which is very questionable.

The legalisation of the rights of the distant needy is underdeveloped. A great deal needs to be aimed for when thinking about the obligations of our legislators, our elected representatives,

---

[78] M Trebilcock, 'The Law and Politics of Immigration Policy' (2003) 5 *American Law and Economics Review* 271.

[79] J Bhagwati, 'Borders Beyond Control' (2003) 82 *Foreign Affairs* 98.

for the protection of the social rights of the global poor. By focusing excessively on justiciability, these great challenges are sometimes left outside the realm of the legal framework. Yet it is crucial to explore the role of human rights in this field. The current institutional framework falls short of an ideal architecture. The incorporation of social rights provisions in the institutional arrangements should form a priority for our legislators and the international community that should aim to make duties towards the distant needy more precise and more effectively delivered.

VII. CONCLUSION

Although you and I might desire different things, we have certain shared fundamental necessities—water, basic nutrition, housing, healthcare, work and others. If these are neglected, we will not be fully human; we will lack dignity; we will be unfree, disrespected and excluded from our community. Because of accidents of history—the Cold War in particular—the current legal framework is characterised by striking weaknesses in the protection of social rights, their scope and the institutional structure. These become particularly acute when compared to the framework for protecting civil and political rights.

In this essay I argued that there is a legal principle that requires the satisfaction of people's basic needs in national and international law. The legalisation of social and economic rights, which encapsulate this principle, should form a priority both at domestic and at international level. Social rights are constitutional essentials at domestic level, as much as civil and political rights are; the two groups of rights are based on common values and have no sharp conceptual differences. Rights to the meeting of basic needs should resist trade-offs and should constitute very weighty considerations for the judiciary when adjudicating, and for the legislature when legislating. The international community and national governments ought to give social rights the urgent attention they deserve when regulating the relationship between the individual and the state, between private individuals, and in reforming the global institutional structure that affects inter-state duties. Some legal orders have made advances that reflect an understanding of the fundamental character of social rights and their importance as a safety net when social structures fail and economic policies lead to destitution. Others have made less progress, and the greatest inadequacies are evident at the global level.

What has been achieved so far in the legal protection of social rights at international and national level, thanks to the moral force and the motivating power of these claims, should not be underestimated. In various countries, the judicial protection of social rights has proven capable of providing an important avenue for the poor and needy, while important academic scholarship has emerged focusing on legislative duties. Yet there are several challenges in legalising social rights: we need further theoretical enquiry into the best institutional arrangements, more empirical research on the potential and practical limitations of the contribution that courts can make, detailed analysis of the remedies that best serve the protection of the rights of the poor, more insistence on the duties of legislatures in protecting social rights, more targeted action to revise our legal framework in a way that takes into account and addresses the suffering of the nearby and the distant needy. The world order should be structured in a way that shows the concern and respect of the affluent for the basic needs of the poor. How this will be achieved is an urgent matter for moral, political and legal argument. In addition, there are questions that this essay did not touch upon at all, as it focused on the law. How should each one of us show concern for the global poor, how should private citizens and civil societies strive to save the lives of those in extreme deprivation? These are important questions with which philosophers and activists are grappling. All these complex matters open up numerous avenues for research and for action.

With their exceptional moral force, social rights provide a starting point that captures the key challenges. They reflect the

[handwritten margin note: Could be achieved at political level]

belief that rights to basic material conditions are universal and have a distinct status. They provide a basis and motivation for improvement of the many shortcomings of the world order; they have potential to inspire and lead social transformation. Reflection on how this will be most effectively achieved through the law is, therefore, a pressing need and a challenge for each one of us interested in a fairer society and a more just world order.

Bibliography

A good starting point is H Steiner, P Alston and R Goodman, *International Human Rights in Context*, 3rd edn (Oxford, Oxford University Press, 2008) chapter 4. This combines legal and theoretical materials and analysis. Several national legal orders protect social rights through different mechanisms: a detailed overview of many of these jurisdictions can be found in M Langford (ed), *Social Rights Jurisprudence* (Cambridge, Cambridge University Press, 2008). Other edited collections that cover a wide variety of social rights and monitoring mechanisms are D Barak-Erez and A Gross (eds), *Exploring Social Rights* (Oxford, Hart Publishing, 2007); B Hepple (ed), *Social and Labour Rights in a Global Context* (Cambridge, Cambridge University Press, 2002); A Eide, K Crause and A Rosas (eds), *Economic, Social and Cultural Rights: A Textbook* (Leiden, Kluwer Law International, 2001).

Good theoretical works on social rights and their correlative duties include H Shue, *Basic Rights*, 2nd edn (Princeton, Princeton University Press, 1996). On moral duties of the affluent towards the needy, see DK Chatterjee (ed), *The Ethics of Assistance: Morality and the Distant Needy* (Cambridge, Cambridge University Press, 2004). Much of the work in this field is concerned with poverty and, in seeking to address this issue, many authors have produced excellent work engaging not just with poverty but with the broader issues as well. See, for example: James Nickel, 'Poverty and Rights' (2005) 55 *Philosophical Quarterly* 385; T Pogge (ed), *Freedom from Poverty as a Human Right: Who Owes What to the Very Poor* (Oxford, OUP, 2007); and in particular the latter author's more recent, 'The Health Impact Fund and its Justification by Appeal to Human Rights' (2009) 40 *Journal of Social Philosophy* 542—an example of activist human rights thinking at its (philosophical) best. D Bilchitz, *Poverty and Fundamental Rights*, (Oxford, Oxford University Press, 2007) is also very rewarding. On global poverty, see C Beitz and

RE Goodin (eds), *Global Basic Rights* (Oxford, Oxford University Press, 2009).

Looking at the broader picture of rights generally, James Nickel, *Making Sense of Human Rights*, 2nd edn (Oxford, Wiley-Blackwell, 2007) contains important analysis of the key issues. Jeremy Waldron's book *Liberal Rights—Collected Papers*, (Cambridge, Cambridge University Press, 1993) contains several important essays on the necessity of social rights. For a philosophical argument for the constitutionalisation of certain social rights, see C Fabre, *Social Rights under the Constitution—Government and the Decent Life* (Oxford, Oxford University Press, 2000). A strand of thinking with which all protagonists for social rights have to deal is libertarianism; in particular R Nozick whose *Anarchy, State and Utopia* (Cambridge, Basic Books, 1974) remains one of the best philosophical arguments for a very limited view of rights. Coming from a traditional conservative position, Maurice Cranston remains highly readable as one of the staunchest opponents of social rights: his *Human Rights To-day* (London, Ampersand, 1962) has been a constant support for those inclined to be antagonistic to what they would describe as over-broad approaches to the subject.

The most interesting example of a country where social rights have been made justiciable is South Africa. The issues in the debate before the enactment of the South African Constitution are analysed in E Mureinik, 'Beyond A Charter of Luxuries: Economic Rights in the Constitution' (1992) 8 *South African Journal of Human Rights* 464; DM Davis, 'The Case Against the Inclusion of Socio-Economic Demands in a Bill of Rights Except As Directive Principles' (1992) 8 *South-African Journal of Human Rights* 475; and C Scott and P Macklem, 'Constitutional Ropes of Sand or Justiciable Guarantees? Social Rights in a New South African Constitution' (1992–1993) 141 *University of Pennsylvania Law Review* 1. More recent literature on the justiciability of social rights in South Africa includes: DM Davis, 'Socio-Economic Rights: Do they Deliver the Goods?' (2008) 6 *International Journal of Constitutional Law* 687; and D Brand and C Heyns (eds), *Socio-*

economic Rights in South Africa (Pretoria, Pretoria University Law Press, 2005). Albie Sachs' autobiographical book *The Strange Alchemy of Life and Law* (Oxford, OUP, 2009) chapter 7, also illustrates the complexities of social rights adjudication. The book by D Bilchitz, *Poverty and Fundamental Rights*, (cited above) discusses the theoretical foundations of social rights and applies the model in South Africa.

There are the beginnings of anxiety about the impact of judge-enforced social rights in South Africa: see J Dugard, 'Judging the Judges: Towards an Appropriate Role for the Judiciary in South Africa's Transformation' (2007) 20 *Leiden Journal of International Law* 965. Much of the literature on social rights does inevitably address this question of justiciability. On different types of judicial review, see M Tushnet, 'Social Welfare Rights and the Forms of Judicial Review' (2003–2004) 82 *Texas Law Review* 1895. A general argument for the justiciability of social rights is to be found in S Fredman, *Human Rights Transformed: Positive Rights, Positive Duties* (Oxford, Oxford University Press, 2008). An important empirical study on the effects of litigation in this field is V Gauri and DM Brinks, *Courting Social Justice* (Cambridge, Cambridge University Press, 2008). See also R Gargarella, P Domingo and T Roux (eds), *Courts and Social Transformation in New Democracies* (Aldershot, Ashgate, 2006). For a sceptical account of the role of courts in Brazil, see O Ferraz, 'The Right to Healthcare in the Courts of Brazil: Worsening Health Inequities?' (2010) 11 *Health and Human Rights* 1. Though no fan of human rights and a noted antagonist of the United Kingdom's Human Rights Act, Keith Ewing has nevertheless argued that without the incorporation of social rights, a constitution is unbalanced: see KD Ewing, 'The Unbalanced Constitution', in T Campbell, K D Ewing, and A Tomkins (eds), *Sceptical Essays on Human Rights* (Oxford, Oxford University Press, 2002) 103. Although, the UK Human Rights Act 1998 does not explicitly guarantee socio-economic rights, it has led to socio-economic issues being raised in the courts. This point has been discussed in E Palmer, *Socio-Economic Rights Adjudication under the Human Rights Act* (Oxford, Hart Publishing, 2007) and in

C O'Cinneide, 'A Modest Proposal: Destitution, State Responsibility and the European Convention on Human Rights' (2008) *European Human Rights Law Review* 583.

US courts have traditionally been hostile towards social rights. This is reflected in the work of Frank Michelman, who has been arguing for the constitutionalisation of social rights for many decades. See for instance, his 'On Protecting the Poor through the Fourteenth Amendment' (1969–1970) 83 *Harvard Law Review* 7. C Sunstein, *The Second Bill of Rights* (Cambridge, Basic Books, 2004) is a characteristically lively contribution from this polymathic author and his *The Costs of Rights—Why Liberty Depends on Taxes* (co-authored with S Holmes) (New York, Norton, 1999) tackles the assumption that freedom of any sort can somehow or other be cost-free. Progressive scholarship in US constitutional law suggests that positive welfare entitlements are and should be a part of the US Constitution, imposing duties not only upon courts but also upon the legislators: see for instance R West, 'Ennobling Politics' in H Jefferson Powell and J Boyd White (eds), *Law and Democracy in the Empire of Force* (Ann Arbor, University of Michigan Press, 2009) 58 and L Sager, *Justice in Plainclothes* (New Haven, Yale University Press, 2004).

Turning now to international law, a good starting point on the UN International Covenant on Economic, Social and Cultural Rights is M Craven, *The International Covenant on Economic, Social and Cultural Rights—A Perspective on its Development* (Oxford, Oxford University Press, 1995). Philip Alston has argued for the necessity to ratify international treaties that protect social rights: see P Alston, 'Putting Economic, Social and Cultural Rights Back on the Agenda of the United States' '(NYU Public Law and Legal Theory Research Paper Series, Working Paper 09-35) available at www.chrgj.org/publications/docs/wp/Alston%20Spring%2009.pdf. Bob Hepple's book *Labour Laws and Global Trade* (Oxford, Hart, 2005) offers a comprehensive overview of the role of different types of transnational regulation in the area of labour rights.

In terms of regional legal orders, so far as Europe is concerned, there are two separate debates, one involving the EU Charter of

Fundamental Rights and the second concerned with the Council of Europe's European Social Charter. The collection of essays, G de Burca and B de Witte (eds), *Social Rights in Europe* (Oxford, Oxford University Press, 2005), covers both jurisdictions. On the protection of social rights in the European Convention on Human Rights, see V Mantouvalou, 'Work and Private Life: Sidabras and Dziautas v Lithuania' (2005) 30 *European Law Review* 573. On the EU Charter of Fundamental Rights, see T Hervey and J Kenner (eds), *Economic and Social Rights under the EU Charter of Fundamental Rights—A Legal Perspective* (Oxford, Hart Publishing, 2003). So far as the Americas are concerned, on the inter-American system, see M Craven, 'The Inter-American System of Human Rights' in DJ Harris and S Livingstone (eds), *The Protection of Economic, Social and Cultural Rights under the Inter-American System of Human Rights* (Oxford, Clarendon, 1998) 289. Finally, on the African Charter of Human and Peoples' Rights, see CA Odinkalu, 'Implementing Economic, Social and Cultural Rights Under the African Charter on Human and Peoples' Rights' in M Evans, R Murray (eds), *The African Charter on Human and Peoples' Rights—The System in Practice 1986–2000* (Cambridge, Cambridge University Press, 2002) 178.

Index